Veloce *Classic Reprint* Series

Volkswagen

The air-cooled era in colour

www.veloce.co.uk

First published in 2005 by Veloce Publishing Limited, Veloce House, Parkway Farm Business Park, Middle Farm Way, Poundbury, Dorchester DT1 3AR, England.
Fax 01305 250479 / e-mail info@veloce.co.uk / web www.veloce.co.uk or www.velocebooks.com
Reprinted June 2017. ISBN 978-1-787111-21-9/UPC 6-36847-01121-5

Veloce *Classic Reprint* Series

Volkswagen
The air-cooled era in colour

Richard Copping

VELOCE PUBLISHING
THE PUBLISHER OF FINE AUTOMOTIVE BOOKS

Contents

www.velocebooks.com

Details all available books • New books • Special offers • Newsletter

Acknowledgements

Four people deserve more than a passing mention for their assistance in helping this book to appear in the form it does. Brian Screaton provided a number of the brochures from which the imagery has been taken. However, more than this, knowing my interest in items relating to the Golden Age, he actively searched out extra goodies for me. Matthew Harrison, who of recent years has been seen at selected events making an honest crust out of re-selling the painstakingly catalogued brochures he's sourced from around the world, went to extraordinary lengths to find items demanded of him, even offering to buy some or all back, if it was so wished, after the book was completed. Vic Kaye presented the contents of his extensive brochure collection for sale, at what it had cost him, when he decided to concentrate his interests elsewhere. Vic also volunteered his services as one with a profound knowledge of the era. Finally, special thanks go to my photographic colleague Ken Cservenka, who proofread the text and due to the nature of the book's make-up, readily agreed to dissolve any unwritten conditions of our Volkswagen partnership.

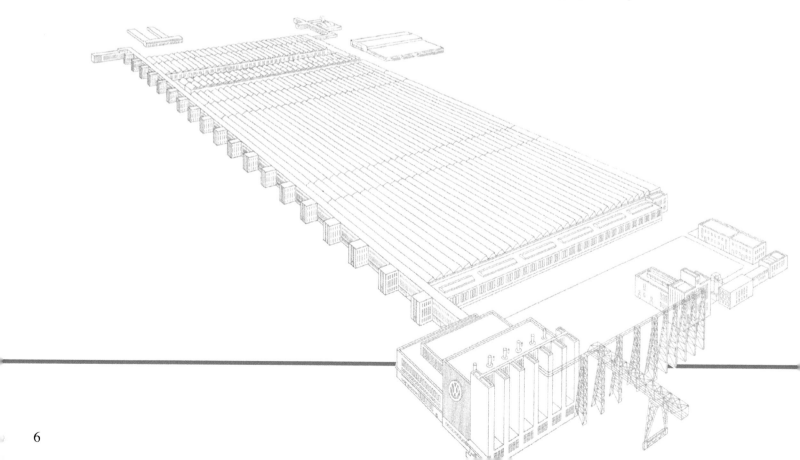

Volkswagen –
the first Golden Age

Car making giant Volkswagen has witnessed peaks and troughs like others of its ilk, but is probably unique in its enjoyment of a first Golden Age which lasted for a full twenty years. Throughout this period (1948 to 1968) there was one man at VW's helm, Heinz Nordhoff, whose pursuit of perfection with the legendary Beetle led to unparalleled success for a single model. However, Nordhoff's Golden Age encompassed far more than the Beetle as other innovative and charismatic models ensured Wolfsburg and its satellites were respected by owners and envied by rival manufacturers right across the world.

Unlike any other volume covering the Volkswagen story, full use has been made of the extensive collection of stunning literature produced to promote and highlight the attributes of the products of the first Golden Age, exactly as the marketing men of the day would have wished. With not a publicity shot in sight, each page of this book is a faithful reproduction, or at least an interpretation, of a leaf from a brochure produced specifically to sell the Volkswagen range. As a result, the book's style divides neatly into two decades each with very different marketing approaches.

Throughout the Fifties, the marketing gurus relied largely on the work of artist Bernd Reuters, whose quest it was to accentuate each Volkswagen's attributes by elongating the vehicles, rounding off any sharp design angles, while reducing the proportions of the apparently well-heeled drivers and passengers, in relation to the size of the cars. Apart from succeeding to great acclaim in this task, Reuters also presented a lasting record of Fifties fashions, attitudes and lifestyles.

With the advent of the Sixties, Volkswagen adopted a dynamically different style of presentation for its products which was uncannily right for the time. Influenced by the recently appointed American advertising agency of Doyle, Dane and Bernbach and with unending cleverness, honesty became Volkswagen's greatest virtue. From stark shots of Volkswagens without a trace of background, to lifestyle images of the products at work in the world at large, this was a style to be lapped up then and equally so, now. The promotional material of this period is really the only such to appear undoctored in this volume.

While it would have been idyllic to take the Volkswagen story on a year-by-year basis from its roots in Nazism, by way of a prelude, to a cursory glance at the last great air-cooled model to come from Wolfsburg as an epilogue to a Golden Age, inevitably under such circumstances, the Beetle would have dominated the pages. Its vast production numbers, its presence from start to finish and its perception then and now, as the model by which Volkswagen either survived, blossomed and flourished, or fell onto hard times, would have ensured this. For this reason, coupled with a desire to satisfy a compartmentalised mind, each Volkswagen model has been allocated its own space, with sufficient room to tell its own story. Theoretically, as a result, it is possible to look at each chapter in isolation without losing the threads of the marketing men's ever-growing web.

Wherever possible, while the text accompanying the original images has been deleted to allow Volkswagen's story to be told, rather than the product promoted, the style, font and layout of the original has been retained. This volume is hopefully an appreciation of the art of marketing and the craft of design, whether the subject matter is the ubiquitous Beetle, the charismatic Transporter, the elegant Karmann Ghia, or the often-overlooked VW 1500 range. The primary intent has been to re-live the years when Nordhoff was in charge and if in so-doing if it becomes apparent that he left Volkswagen in a strong position, with an unfolding range of updated and new products, it will have served to remind readers that Volkswagen would have remained prosperous into the Seventies had he lived.

Richard A Copping

Heinz Nordhoff, 6 January, 1899 - 12 April, 1968
Volkswagen's director general from his appointment in January 1948, until his death a little over twenty years later.

It was thanks to his unstinting devotion to his products and his total belief in their durability that Volkswagen's first Golden Age endured so long.

Volkswagen – The People´s Car

Dark preamble to a Golden Age

That the birth of Volkswagen is inextricably linked with the rise of Nazism is an inescapable fact, however unpalatable. While Ferdinand Porsche had made numerous attempts to fulfil one of his lifelong ambitions of creating an affordable car for the people, each had ended in failure. Greater potential financial reward in other areas and curious treaties between manufacturers might have been the underlying causes, rather than fundamental flaws in Porsche's designs, but without the financial backing required the result was the same.

Only twelve days after his appointment as Germany's chancellor, Hitler spoke at the opening of the 1933 Berlin Auto Show. His message was one of mass mobilisation, tax abatements for car owners and the building of the autobahns - music to the ears of many, including Ferdinand Porsche. The notion of a people's car became red hot in the press, while Porsche beavered away on the production of a paper entitled *Ideas on the Design and Construction of a German People's Car*. This was presented to the Reich Ministry of Transport on January 17 1934 and the rest, as they say, is history; almost.

Without Hitler's power to quash all opposition, it's fair to assume that the Volkswagen's road to production would have been rutted with potholes. Naturally, established manufacturers had more than a vested interest in the success of their own models. Having involved themselves in the process of producing a people's car, obstacles soon appeared. The Nazi regime would not be denied. Years later, the chief engineer of Volkswagen's first Golden Age, Heinz Nordhoff, was to say that 'without question, Porsche led a fight against the entire German car industry ... A secret underground fight, of course,

and one which ended to his and the Volkswagen's benefit, only because Hitler stood behind the entire plan'. Employed by, and loyal to, Opel at the time, even Nordhoff's reaction to the Volkswagen was described as 'completely disdainful' by someone who was to work with him many years later.

Hitler's ruthlessness in pursuit of his automotive goals was demonstrated on two occasions. On February 28 1937, he opened the Berlin Motor Show once more. 'Let there be no doubt,' he told the world, 'so-called private business is either capable of solving this problem [of producing a Volksauto], or it is not capable of continuing as private business. The National Socialist State will under no circumstances capitulate before either the inconvenience, the limitations, or the ill-will of individual Germans.' At the same event, von Opel showed Hitler his latest car, the P-4, 'the motor car for the little man'. Immediately, Hitler arranged that it become difficult for manufacturers to obtain the materials they needed to build such vehicles, while von Opel was told unofficially that his suggested cut in the vehicle's price would not be allowed. No German car would be permitted to compete with the Volkswagen.

In late May 1937, the Nazis formed the Gessellschaft zur Vorbereitung des Volkswagens, or the Volkswagen Development Company. Initially capitalised with 480,000 marks, investment increased to 150 million mark in July 1939. Inextricably linked to the German Labour Front, indirectly this meant the Volkswagen had at its disposal the funds of the German government. The next stage was building a massive factory on virgin land in which to manufacture the Volksauto. Never before or since has a car had such a start in life.

Marketing the Strength Through Joy Car

Plans for the Volkswagen were such that 100,000 cars were to be built in 1940, increasing year by year until the point full production was achieved in 1944, at a total of 450,000 Volksautos per annum. Although these figures were later revised, a marketing strategy had to be devised to 'sell' the car that Hitler would officially name as the Kraft-durch-Freude Wagen, or Strength through Joy Car, at the factory foundation stone laying ceremony. (By so doing, Hitler linked it even more firmly with the German Labour Front and its KdF subsidiary, which organised all leisure time activities.) Labour Front leader Robert Ley, who devised a unique opportunity for all to purchase a Volkswagen, was only too aware of the magnitude of his task. Launching a 5-mark-a-month layaway scheme on August 1 1938, he declared that 'it is the Fuhrer's will that within a few years no less than 6,000,000 Volkswagens will be on German roads. In 10 years' time, there will be no working person in Germany who does not own a "people's car".'

A colourfully covered brochure packed with carefully posed photographs, each intended to convey the many advantages of owning a Volkswagen, rapidly appeared, as did a complete A to Z handbook. The brochure particularly sold the layaway scheme to perfection, with 336,668 would-be owners having signed up by 1940. Of these savers, 70 per cent had never owned a car before, while 40,000 aspired to move up from life as motorcyclists. Some 50 per cent of the savers earned less than 300 marks monthly, and without the scheme couldn't have contemplated owning a motorcar.

Hitler's ambitions as a world leader, and the inevitable spiral into war, meant that only a handful of Volkswagens were built before and during those dark destructive times. Of the few that were completed, none reached ordinary Germans, being reserved in the main for high-ranking members of the Nazi party.

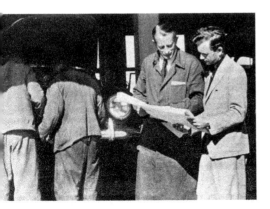

With the Volkswagen's mentors swept away by the Allies, its story might have been over. A series of remarkable coincidences saved it. Although the Americans rescued the 'inhabitants' of the factory, it was positioned in the British area of control. A British officer, Major Ivan Hirst, was given the task of acting as caretaker to the wreckage of the ownerless factory until its fate was decided. Thanks to its 'private' Nazi rather than military past, the buildings were saved from summary demolition.

However, as the factory hadn't been operational before 1939, it was classed as surplus to the proposed post war level of German industry and, as such, subject to reparations, or dismantling, with its effects distributed amongst the Allies.

Hirst's recognition of the need for transport among military personnel and, ironically, his determination to build the wartime derivative of the Volkswagen, the Kübelwagen, saved both the factory and the car. It was Ambi-Budd of Berlin that had built Kübel bodies, but its factory had been so badly damaged that only a few body dies remained while, thanks to its location in the Soviet sector, co-operation was strictly limited. Hirst reluctantly turned to the saloon.

Having successfully achieved production, albeit in relatively low numbers, whilst various reparation groups and well-known car manufacturers turned their backs on the product, the British planned handover to the German people had to be backed by a long-term management strategy. The German 'receiver' at Wolfsburg, Hermann Munch, lacked a motor industry backgroung and was unsuitable for a managerial role. Heinz Nordhoff, a former director of Opel, couldn't return there, partly due to a minor honour received from the Nazis. His appointment as Volkswagen's general manager with effect from January 1948 was an inspired choice. That he insisted on being his own man from the start ensured his position, while his determination to succeed led to the re-founding of Volkswagen as a brand, with the launch of a totally revitalised car in the summer of 1949.

Specifically designed to cater to the tastes of customers in markets other than Germany, the Export, or Deluxe, Volkswagen was launched in July 1949, at a cost of 5450DM. Easily distinguishable from earlier examples by its abundance of chrome and bright work, which even extended to the car's running boards, its interior fittings were of better quality, while the upholstery was also substantially upgraded. Equally key to the model's success was the availability for the first time of high-gloss paintwork. Mechanically, the 'new' car was identical to its predecessor, which remained in production, albeit re-branded as the 'Standard'. Cable brakes and a crash box were hallmarks of all Volkswagens until April 1950 and October 1952 respectively.

Belonging to Porsche's original line-up, the sunroof model depicted above was added to the post war range at the end of April 1950. The extra cost amounted to 250DM and – like the prototypes from over a decade before – the canvas roof concertinaed back on itself to leave a good proportion of the interior exposed to the elements.

Engine:	Four cylinder, horizontally opposed, air-cooled
Valves:	Overhead, central camshaft
Cubic capacity:	1131cc (until December 1953)
Displacement:	25bhp at 3300rpm
Bore and stroke:	75mm bore, 64mm stroke
Compression ratio:	5.8:1
Carburettor:	Single Solex (26VFIS to Oct 52, then 28PCI)
Oil capacity:	4.4imp pints
Drive:	Rear wheels
Transmission:	4 forward speeds, 1 reverse (synchromesh on second, third and fourth from Oct 1952, export model only)
Brakes:	cable operated until mid-1950, then hydraulic (not standard model)
Tyres:	5.00 x 16in (From October 1952, 5.60 x 15in)
Chassis/frame:	Channel shaped centre section, forked at the rear and welded-on platforms
Front axle:	Independent suspension via transversely mounted torsion bars
Rear axle:	Swinging half axles, with spring plates and torsion bars
Steering:	Transverse link with unequal length track rods – worm and nut
Overall dimensions:	Length 4070mm, width 1540mm, height 1500mm
Weight:	730kg
General data:	Principal paint options (1950 – export) Pastel Green, Middle Brown, Bordeaux Red, Black Weatherproof synthetic resin finish

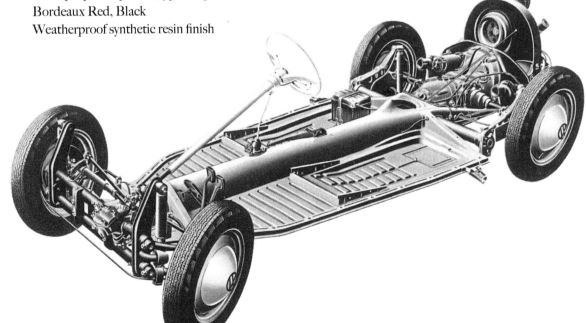

VOLKSWAGEN BEETLE

It was at the beginning of the fifties that Volkswagen adopted the artwork of Bernd Reuters.

Reuters elongated the look of the Beetle, making it appear a faster, more expensive and desirable car than any photograph could.

Until the arrival of the Transporter in March 1950, the Volkswagen Sedan, plus its exclusive soft top option, was the factory's only product. From that point, although Volkswagen continued to refer to the car as the Volkswagen, for modern eyes and ears it is preferable to adopt the nickname that many years later Volkswagen would acknowledge - the Beetle.

When questioned, Volkswagen today seem to know little about Bernd Reuters, which is a shame, as material featuring his work consistently outsells later artwork. Inevitably, such brochures command premium prices.

Production figures rose increasingly year on year. In 1949, 46,154 cars were produced, the majority of which rolled off the assembly line after the introduction of the Export model. In 1950, the figure had jumped to 81,979, follwed by 93,709 in 1951. In 1952, the 100,000 barrier in a twelve month period was broken with 114,348 cars, while the following year over 151,000 cars were produced.

Until March 1953, the Beetle was instantly recognisable by its split rear screen, a measure originally employed for reasons of cost and technology, as two small flat panes of glass were less expensive than one curved larger piece - something which had only just begun to appear on the market.

1951 saw the 250,000 Beetle to be built since the end of the war. Business was booming as Nordhoff triumphantly conquered one export market after another. Countries succumbing to the Beetle's charms included Denmark, Luxembourg, Sweden, Switzerland and Belgium, but one market eluded Volkswagen for a little longer. Beetle sales in the USA, even as late as 1952, totalled less than 1000 cars, out of annual car purchases across the country amounting to close on 7 million. Sales revenue had jumped from 243 million DM in 1949, to 660 million, making future investments possible.

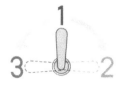

A Volkswagen with a difference

As far back as the foundation stone laying ceremony in 1938, a convertible version of the car had been envisaged. In the brief post war interlude of British control, various prototypes had been built with varying degrees of success. One such, nicknamed the 'Radclyffe Roadster' after Hirst's superior officer, to whom it was 'donated', met with particular acclaim. Nordhoff, however, had neither the available labour nor the free capacity to contemplate such a low volume addition to his range.

Two coach-building firms were eager to muscle in on the act - Osnabruck and Joseph Hebmüller. Both had already produced prototypes

after obtaining Beetles on which to experiment. Wilhelm Karmann, of the Osnabruck coach-building firm, established as long ago as 1874, was given the go-ahead for his third prototype by Nordhoff in the latter part of 1948, following an increase in the availability of raw materials. The four-seater Cabriolet, heavily reinforced with strengthening members under each sill and supports around the doors to prevent flexing, was ready for inspection in May 1949. Extensive testing of 25 pre-production models was soon underway, and in late August Nordhoff ordered 2000 cars. Production started in September, at a rate varying between one and two cars per day. By December, this figure had increased to six per day.

A Car with a Difference – But still a True Volkswagen

The Wuppertal-based firm of Joseph Hebmüller had been creating convertibles out of saloon cars since 1919. In 1948, it built three prototype two-seater cabriolets, their most distinctive feature being what, at first glance, appeared to be a rear engine cover based on the car's boot lid.

As with Karmann's product, flexing proved the biggest headache and similar techniques to those used by the Osnabruck firm were employed to overcome the issue. After extensive testing, the first cars were produced in June 1949, following Volkswagen's first order for 2000 examples. Sadly, fire spread through the Hebmüller factory on July 23 1949, and, while production restarted, it soon became apparent that the firm had severe financial problems. Amazingly, it wasn't until 1952 that the company finally registered itself bankrupt. This marked the end of what was undoubtedly the most elegant of Volkswagen Cabriolets.

Utilising many components supplied by Wolfsburg, nevertheless new panels had to be grafted onto the body to give the Cabriolet its unique qualities and to allow for rear side windows, which could be lowered. Considerable strengthening of the sills and other areas already mentioned also took time for Karmann's skilled workforce to achieve. Even the engine lid had to be modified, as the air inlets positioned just below the rear window on the Sedan had to be moved further down to save partial obliteration from Karmann's hood when lowered. The result was a near hand-built and certainly hand-finished car, crowned with a top that took two men four hours to install. Consisting of three layers, the hood had a woollen roof-liner and horsehair padding, topped off with a waterproof linen skin. Unusually for the time, the tiny rear window (increased in size in 1952 and again in 1958) was made of glass, while the top was firmly secured to a complicated combination of wood and steel, which formed the frame. The Cabriolet's

launch price reflected the work involved to create it. At 7500DM, it was nearly 40 per cent more expensive than the Export model, which cost 5450DM.

From the start the Cabriolet was based on the most luxurious version of the Beetle. Initially this was a straightforward decision to make, as there were only the Export and Standard models to choose between. Towards the end of Volkswagen's first Golden Age, the Cabriolet was based on both the 1300 Beetle and, subsequently, the 1500.

Heralding unrivalled triumphs

March 1953 heralded a major advance for the Beetle, coming from a change in appearance that seemed trivial compared to previous modifications. From the tenth of the month, Beetles featured a single oval-shaped pane of glass in the rear window, increasing the size by 23 per cent. Despite a major revamping of the car in October 1952 – a redesigned dashboard had been installed; new sturdier chrome bumpers had been fitted; additional bright-work had become a feature; smaller chunkier tyres had appeared and synchromesh had made its debut – it was the single act of cutting out a small strip of metal six months later that made the car appear far less Teutonic.

In July, Volkswagen's workforce celebrated the arrival of the 500,000 Beetle, receiving a bonus totalling 2.5 million DM, while Nordhoff had already established Volkswagen do Brasil, for the assembly and later manufacture of Beetles (and Transporters) in South America. Britain too received its first official quota of the cars and although the franchise made a loss in its first year of trading, this was another significant pocket of resistance broken.

At the end of 1953, the Beetle's engine performance was increased from 25 to 30bhp, or from 1131 to 1192cc. The compression ratio rose from 5.8:1 to 6.1:1. The net result of these advances was that the Beetle was now capable of a cruising and maximum speed of 68mph.

Nordhoff, who had once described the Beetle as having 'more defects than a dog has fleas', had turned the car's fortunes around completely. Such was his genius that he was alleged to have said with confidence that 'Germany should go where Volkswagen leads it, not the other way around.' Nordhoff had a growing conviction that his blessings lay 'not in bolder and more magnificent designs, but in the consistent and tireless redevelopment of every tiny detail until perfection is achieved, which is the mark of a really outstanding car and which brings astonishing success ... [The Beetle] holds the number one position in the whole of the European car industry ... We sell the Volkswagen in those countries with a large, competitive and from our side highly respected car industry, with one single argument only: quality!' Such sentiments were to be a recurring theme throughout his life.

The occasion, on the afternoon of August 5 1955, of the birth of the millionth Beetle was one of the utmost significance to Volkswagen, and heralded unprecedented festivities. While in later years it has been cynically suggested that the ceremonies were an important part of a self-inspired, gigantic public relations exercise, intended to achieve near deification for Nordhoff, such sentiments only tend to be uttered by those with a particular plot to weave: one intended to deny Volkswagen's air-cooled heritage and refute the notion of a first Golden Age.

To the accompaniment of Parisian dancers from the Moulin Rouge, tartan-clad Scottish girls and their bagpipes, a troupe of flag-waving Swiss nationals and a melodic South African choir, whose spirituals echoed around the halls of Wolfsburg, Heinz Nordhoff addressed an admiring and jubilant audience. 'These celebrations', he said, 'have provided a glimpse of the world which the Volkswagen has conquered and will continue to conquer'.

That the director general had more than one motive in achieving the magic one million figure with the car that had been rescued by the British from the ashes of Nazism cannot be denied, but none related to self-glorification. Instead, Nordhoff had been determined to restore Germany's stature in the eyes

of the world through the Beetle. In his first year in charge, he had pledged that 'it will be up to us to build this, the biggest car factory in Germany into a decisive factor in the German peacetime economy.'

During Nordhoff's triumphal address of August 1955, to a vast assembly totalling some 160,000 dignitaries, international motoring correspondents, journalists and countless Volkswagen distributorships and dealers, the theme of world conquest through 'hard work and determination' became increasingly apparent. While the home market might yet remain the largest, the desire to distribute Beetles wherever the car was accepted and – more importantly – where at first it wasn't, was obvious. In the mid-fifties, exports accounted for 55 per cent of total production. For Nordhoff, in a post war Europe dominated by long established and highly respected motoring marques, the achievement of being the first and youngest factory to produce one million cars of the same type was paramount.

In 1948, Nordhoff declared, Volkswagen had 40 distributors in Germany and one abroad. Now, there were 1000 in Germany and over 2800 elsewhere. Exports had risen dramatically from humble origins, so that in 1955, 28,000 cars would be despatched to Sweden, 18,000 to Belgium, 14,000 to Holland and 10,000 to Austria. The most commendable achievement of all centred round the all-important USA, where from a reluctance to accept even two cars in the late forties, sales had rocketed to 35,000 per annum by 1955.

400,000 of Nordhoff's first million cars went abroad, with 103 countries succumbing to the Teutonic presence of Germany's Beetle and with the promise of more, much more to come. The marketing men were tasked with the job of translating Volkswagen's benchmark slogan of 'Es lohnt sich, auf einen Volkswagen zu warten', (A Volkswagen is worth waiting for) into every conceivable language.

Invitee and British motoring journalist, Bill Boddy, prepared a lengthy account of what he had witnessed at Wolfsburg in the high summer of 1955, concluding that, while he had 'no reason to be frantically pro-German', he would be 'sub-human if this journey to Wolfsburg had left me unimpressed.'

Other celebrations would follow as Beetle sales continued to escalate – the two-millionth car arrived less than three years later – but none would epitomise Volkswagen's first Golden Age more.

As the millionth Beetle was rolling off the assembly line, something else of significance was happening at Wolfsburg. After working to a rather ad hoc arrangement of calendar years more or less coinciding with model years, with effect from August 1955, cars built after the annual factory holiday shutdown were deemed to belong to the 'next' year. Hence, a car built in August 1955, was one of the first '56 model year Beetles. A pattern was introduced of coinciding any major changes with this magical cut-off point. 1956 Beetles were a striking example of the new policy, in that cars built after the holidays featured a redesigned rear valance, built to accommodate a new silencer, complete with twin tailpipes. New rear-light clusters were positioned higher on the car's wings, while inside, a whole host of tweaks improved both the driver's and the passengers' lot.

In October 1955, Volkswagen of America Inc was founded, a body that would prove ruthlessly effective in setting benchmarks for US dealers, weeding out those whose standards in service requirements left even a little to be desired. US sales continued to rise, with more and more consignments of cars finding their way across the Atlantic. The key to US success had been a somewhat haphazard campaign of attracting business through two dynamic individuals, Gottfried Lange and Will Van de Kamp, who had carved the USA into western and eastern territories. Now with a more disciplined structure settled, the maverick Van de Kamp was gently eased out of his role, to be replaced by a man with a feeling for marketing and promotional activities. This man was Carl Hahn, Nordhoff's one-time personal assistant and a future director general of Volkswagen.

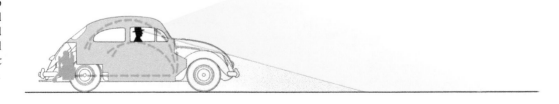

August 1957 proved a big moment in the history of the Beetle. With the arrival of the new model year cars, its looks were transformed. Such was the dramatic increase in the size of the rear window that Bernd Reuters was commissioned to prepare a previously unheard of brochure front cover depicting the car 'driving' into the distance. The intention was clear: Volkswagen, the least extravagantly showy of car manufacturers, had something to shout about. Additionally, such was the Beetle's status in the world that it was unnecessary to include more than the legendary 'V' over 'W' on the page by way of description.

While Volkswagen was wise to emphasise the increase in glass size as a hook to catch additional buyers, another change occurred in August 1957, one that would remain with the Beetle to the very end of production over 45 years later. Gone was the enticing dashboard that had first appeared in October 1952, to be replaced by something even better and which soon became widely regarded as the most aesthetically pleasing option of all. Although Nordhoff and his closest colleagues resisted the influence of 'hysterical stylists', all of them appreciated the clever nature of the design, with the glovebox lid shaped to match two grilles surrounding the car's single dial. Behind the larger of these there was space to locate a speaker for the radio, which in turn sat elegantly and accessibly in the centre of the dash.

The copywriters described the interior of the Volkswagen as 'both handsome and functional'. Curiously, having carefully turned the car around to display its biggest feature, little text was used to discuss a rear window glass increased by nearly 95 per cent at, not to mention the 17 per cent enlargement at the front. Perhaps following the lead set by Volkswagen, *The Autocar* underplayed the car's new assets when it came to review the product in December 1957. While concluding that the Volkswagen had set 'new standards for the motor trade', the increases in glass size were referred to in the most factual of ways and it was almost casually admitted that the 'facia' had been redesigned 'in the interest of appearance'. However, Nordhoff's policy of disallowing change for change's sake was well and truly vindicated when, in December 1957, the two-millionth Beetle rolled off the assembly line.

More Power for a New Decade

Although the 1961 model Beetle looked quite similar externally (a notable exception being the introduction, finally, of wing mounted indicators in place of the antiquated semaphores which other manufacturers had abandoned many years earlier), the car was very much an improved product.

Four more horses for *the Volkswagen*

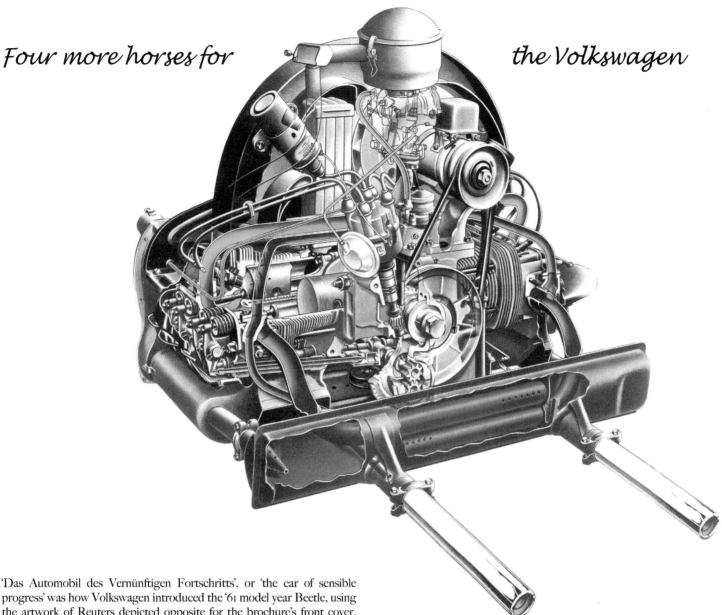

'Das Automobil des Vernünftigen Fortschritts', or 'the car of sensible progress' was how Volkswagen introduced the '61 model year Beetle, using the artwork of Reuters depicted opposite for the brochure's front cover. Although the marketing men went on to itemise 30 different improvements, by far the most important was the new engine, which was mated to a fully synchronised box.

The 34bhp engine, which, with very little tweaking, would remain familiar to the Beetle until the mid-eighties, had already been dropped into the Transporter. Although it retained a capacity of 1192cc, more power was available due to numerous detail changes and an increase in compression ratio from 6.6:1 to 7.0:1. Very few parts were interchangeable with those of the old 30bhp engine, which remained in production specifically for would be owners of the Standard model. The modifications made included: a stronger crankshaft and a more rugged crankcase; redesigned cylinder heads; greater spacing of the cylinder barrels and a detachable dynamo pedestal. Volkswagen claimed a conservative increase in top speed of 5km/h for the new engine, but also admitted that fuel consumption was a little heavier. Although petrol prices weren't an issue in 1960, some were ready to blame the newly arrived, thermostatically controlled, automatic choke for this. To aid cold starting, a flexible hose was fitted to the left-hand heat exchanger, its purpose being to direct warm air from the exchanger onto the air cleaner and over the carburettor.

A Beetle FOR THE SIXTIES

'A 10 per cent increase in power output has raised the top speed to just under 72mph and in conjunction with a final drive ratio lowered by about 7 per cent, has substantially improved acceleration figures. ... Everything about [the Beetle] ... is sensibly designed, well made and carefully finished. Solid construction, materials and equipment selected for toughness, long life and suitability for purpose, and excellent paintwork, all add to the general impression of engineering integrity.' *The Motor*, October 5 1960.

The US market had rid itself of the semaphores in the mid-fifties when special cone-shaped indicators were positioned close to the Beetle's headlamps. For the '58 model year, US indicators took up what would soon be a familiar stance on the top of the wings. Why Volkswagen clung on to the semaphore in Europe to the end of the decade remains a mystery. Although the '61 model saw many improvements, one anomaly remained: a complete and utter reliance on a reserve fuel tap. Virtually all other manufactures provided even their budget-range cars with a petrol gauge.

It was with the introduction of the 34bhp engine that Volkswagen lifted the aesthetic standard to even loftier heights. Matching and toning colours became a high priority, which on occasion appeared to be taken to hardly cost-effective extremes. For example, a car finished in Beryl Green also included a colour-coded steering wheel and gearlever, as well as matching rubber mats and tunnel covers – a nightmare for today's owners if the product is ever damaged. Externally, even the running boards received the same colour treatment.

Onwards and upwards

By 1960, for the first time, Volkswagen had almost caught up with the ever-increasing demand for Beetles. Massive investment had been, and would continue to be, the key. The year the millionth Beetle rolled off the assembly line, there were 279,986 cars produced and investments of 173 million DM. In 1957 – the year of the two-millionth – there were 380,561 produced, and 575,407 two years after that, when the third-millionth hit the streets. In 1960, there were 739,455 Beetles produced and investments had soared to 465 million DM. Nordhoff's Volkswagen was moving forwards in leaps and bounds. The opportunity at last arose to expand the product base, leading to the introduction in late 1961 of a larger family saloon, the VW 1500. However, the drive to produce and sell even more Beetles was never lost.

With the artwork produced for the '61 model year (see pages 26 to 29), Volkswagen said a fond farewell to Bernd Reuters, opting instead to entice buyers with a variety of photographs, ranging from simplistic vehicle shots to exotic lifestyle poses. Hence, while the work of Reuters accompanies the Transporter, Beetle-based Karmann Ghia Coupé and the Cabriolet, the VW 1500 range was launched on the back of photographs, which to some of today's enthusiasts are almost as fascinating. In the USA, a series of groundbreaking adverts were in their infancy as the new decade started to mature. While having a dramatic outcome on sales, they would also soon influence Volkswagen's photographic statements across the world.

Crucial to an understanding of the Beetle's advancement in the sixties is an appreciation of Nordhoff's philosophy. As the decade moved forwards, his pronouncements were heard with increasing frequency. The message had always been there; it simply became more important as the Beetle matured past an age where many other manufacturers' models would have already been consigned to the scrapheap, whatever their merits. Speaking on November 13 1958, on the occasion of his presentation with the USA's prestigious Elmer A Sperry award, Nordhoff summarised his beliefs. 'I brushed away all of the temptations to change model and design. In any sound design there are almost unlimited possibilities – and this [the Beetle's], certainly was a sound one. I see no sense in starting anew every few years with the same teething troubles, making

obsolete almost all the past. I went out on a limb. I took the chance of breaking away from the beaten path ... Offering people an honest value, a product of the highest quality, with low original cost and incomparable re-sale value, appealed more to me than being driven by a bunch of hysterical stylists trying to sell people something they really do not want to have. And still it does! Improving quality and value steadily, without increasing price ... simplifying and intensifying service and spare parts systems, building a product of which I and every other Volkswagen worker can be truly proud ... I am firmly convinced that there will always be a market in this world, which we are far from covering now, for simple, economical and dependable transportation and for an honest value in performance and in quality. I am convinced that, all over the world ... there are millions of people who will gladly exchange chromium plated gadgets and excessive power for economy, long life and inexpensive maintenance. So I have decided to stick to the policy that has served us so well. Based on Professor Porsche's original design, the Volkswagen of today looks almost exactly like the prototype model that was produced more than twenty years ago, but every single part of this car has been refined and improved over the years – these will continue to be our 'model changes'. This policy has required, of course, a great deal in the way of determination and courage, on the part of myself and the members of our organisation. But it has led to success and there is no greater justification than success, as every engineer will agree.'

Five million define the goal

After cheering along the four-millionth Beetle on November 9 1960, Nordhoff was ready to present the flower-bedecked fifth just over a year later, on December 5 1961. On this occasion, the lucky recipient of the car was the International Red Cross.

Here was another opportunity for Nordhoff to reiterate Volkswagen's philosophy. The Beetle, proclaimed the director general, was 'a symbol of hard, unremitting work and of diligent attention to a correctly set goal', while the creed was: '... to develop one model of car to its highest technical excellence ... to dedicate ourselves to the attainment of the highest quality ... to destroy the notion that such high quality can only be attained at high prices ... [and] to give the car the highest value and to build it so that it retains that value ...' The golden age of the fifties for the Beetle, and therefore for Volkswagen, was set to continue.

In 1961, 827,850 Beetles were produced which, with a little help from the Transporter, generated 4423 million DM in sales revenue, accounted for a massive 596 million DM in investments and returned a profit of 71.9 million DM. The Volkswagenwerk was already Germany's leading commercial venture, and now it became the world's third-largest car manufacturer, behind US giants General Motors and Ford, respectively. By 1961, Wolfsburg housed 10,000 production machines and covered 10 million sq ft.

By 1963, when the photographs reproduced here were released, what had once been a limited partnership was now most clearly a company, the Volkswagenwerk Aktiengesellschaft Wolfsburg.

Until the Allied victory in 1945, the Strength through Joy factory and the products it should have been producing were in the ownership of the Nazi party. During the British period of control the by-then ownerless factory was requisitioned by the military government and a custodian, or receiver, was appointed. In 1949, the chairman of the board of trustees, Colonel Charles Radclyffe, signed over the factory to German ownership once more. The federal government received the assets of the former Nazi enterprise and disposed of them in accordance with the relevant articles of the Bonn constitution. The province of Lower Saxony, in whose boundaries the Volkswagenwerk lay, was appointed to manage government interests. In June 1959, after much wrangling, the federal government and its appointee effectively changed Volkswagen from a limited partnership to a share issuing limited company.

Volkswagen was floated on the stock exchange on August 22 1960, although Bonn and Lower Saxony retained a 20 per cent holding each. In July 1961, the first annual meeting of shareholders was held, where a dividend of 12 per cent was announced for the 1960 trading year.

Although the images of the '63 model depict a car apparently identical to the Beetle of 1961, improvements had been made, as was the norm for Volkswagen. By the start of the '62 model year, a separate section of amber plastic in the larger, rear light housing distinguished the indicator from other functions. In August 1961, the Beetle finally received a fuel gauge. Sadly, from October 1962, just two months into the lifespan of the 1963 model, the elegant Wolfsburg badge above the boot lid handle had been removed. On the plus side, a perforated plastic headlining gave the car a light and airy feeling when compared to the older woollen item. Most important though was the introduction of heat exchangers. These ensured odourless warm air, when required, in both the front and back of the car's interior.

Why Volkswagen offered Beetles at discounted prices

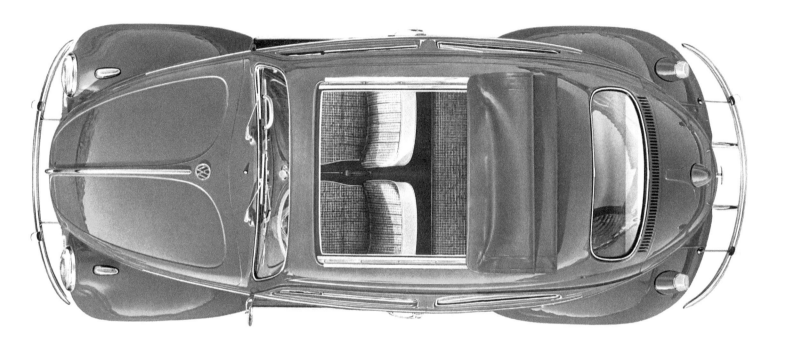

Under the terms of the Nazi Savings Scheme, 336,638 people had set aside monies to become KdF-Wagen owners, their money being deposited in the Bank of German Labour. Although the funds were intact at the end of the war, advancing Soviet forces took all they found. In 1948, the 'Association of Former VW Savers' was established, with the intention of using the courts to acquire a brand-new Beetle for every claimant. Two years later the claimants hopes were dashed, when a ruling found the Volkswagenwerk to be contractual partners, but not responsible for fulfilment of the original pledge. In 1954, the courts ruled that the Nazi Labour Front was actually the Savers' true partner, and absolved the post war Volkswagen factory of any responsibility. Volkswagen met with the Savers' leader in both 1956 and 1958, but with no result. Finally, in 1961, a deal emerged that was deemed satisfactory by all. Those savers who had completed their payments were to receive either 100DM in cash, or a discount of 600DM on the price of a new car (by this time the Deluxe Beetle cost 4740DM).

By mid-1964, some 93,000 savers had submitted their claims and 87,000 were upheld. Surprisingly, only 50 per cent opted for a discount.

In 1963, Beetle production fell for the first time since Volkswagen was returned to German control. The total number of cars produced dropped from 877,014 in 1962, to 838,488. Certainly on the home market both Ford and Opel had signalled their intention to close the gap, with the introduction of new models offering more space and performance. However, their efforts still left Beetle sales accounting for double that of any other single product. Perhaps the critics had failed to consider the effect of the marketing campaign for the recently introduced, larger VW 1500, a model that Beetle owners could aspire to. Production of that vehicle rose by 54,485 cars in the same year (the Beetle had correspondingly dropped by 38,526 cars). In any event, 1963 has to be seen as a minor anomaly in the Beetle's history, as the following year production shot up to 948,370 cars. No discount deals to be done here, then!

Automation

As Beetle production continued to escalate and labour shortages became increasingly apparent, streamlining and automation grew to be essential. In 1958, 39,794 people on the shop floor had totted up 553,399 vehicles. Five years later, 72,887 Volkswagen workers in Germany produced 1,132,080 cars. Admittedly the Transporter was involved throughout and, in 1963, the VW 1500 had joined the act, but the main thrust was, and would remain, the Beetle. In 1958, each worker knitted together an average of 13.9 Volkswagens, whereas in 1963, this figure had risen to 15.5. At nearly 73,000 workers, more labour could still be found and would be, but modernising production methods was clearly the way forward. A new, 180-metre-long assembly line was duly installed at Wolfsburg, which managed sixteen different operations and was capable of producing 3300 cars daily from a two-shift operation. Having set the ball rolling, 57 additional presses were built to keep the assembly line supplied with sufficient body parts. Even the paint department had to be upgraded as a result, with the addition of two more lines.

Set alongside the words of a modern-day marketing guru, Volkswagen's advertising stance of the fifties simply wouldn't stand a chance. 'Car ads of the day were campy, unrealistic looking things, with illustrations rather than photographs. This allowed artists to exaggerate features. People depicted in the ads were drawn out of scale, shown smaller than in life compared to the car. Sunbursts, little jewel-like explosions of light, were drawn in to illuminate the precious value of the car. It was all dishonest and false.' So wrote David Kiley in his highly entertaining and informative volume, *Getting the Bugs Out*. While today we can drool over Reuters' period artwork and pay big money to become owners of some of 'his' brochures, it was through the work of one dynamic US advertising

The DDB factor

a handful of 'home-grown' small cars were scheduled for release in 1959. The time had to be right to advertise aggressively, despite Beetle sales topping the 80,000 mark in 1958 and not to mention a six month waiting list to get hold of one. Hahn challenged more than a dozen agencies with the question of how they would sell the Beetle. A young company of just ten years' standing, already renowned for both creative and unusual work, had the answer.

Doyle, Dane Bernbach Inc, led by Bill Bernbach, who was described as the 'inspiration' of many another, presented un-doctored photos, covered just one theme in an advertisement, chose not to do the traditional thing of having a dig at Detroit and didn't even try to sell cars. What DDB did do was to ensure that its advertisements for Volkswagen were both seen and read. From Bernbach's very first, with the one line message 'Why do people wait six months for a VW when they can have any other car immediately', which was later simplified to 'Why are people buying Volkswagens faster than they can be made', DDB pitched it just right. Whether the Beetle reached cult status in the States as a result of DDB's spell is open to question, but what is certain is that it certainly didn't detract from it. Within a few years, Volkswagen was using DDB in many markets, including all the main satellites, plus Britain, France, Spain, Italy and not un-naturally Germany itself. Such was DDB's influence that whole brochures might be compiled of little more than a string of the most subtly honest of advertisements.

As a tribute to the skill of DDB and the added impetus it put into Beetle sales, turn the page to find just about the only style of brochure page reproduced without any form of alteration.

agency that Volkswagen not only multiplied sales many times over, but also stole a considerable march on would-be competitors. The name of the game was honesty. Nobody had thought of it before. Car salesmen and honesty, dare it be said, don't necessarily gel!

Nordhoff protégé and recently appointed Volkswagen chief in the USA, Carl Hahn, was aware that more than

You're missing a lot when you own a Volkswagen.

A VW has fewer parts than other cars because it needs fewer parts.

It doesn't need a drive shaft to transfer engine power to the rear wheels. Because our car's engine is in back to start with (and to maintain traction with).

And it doesn't need a radiator, or a water pump, or hoses. Because the engine's cooled with air, not water.

(When you drive your first VW, you may miss putting in antifreeze, rust inhibitors and whatnot. But you'll soon get used to it.)

The stuff a VW doesn't use, it doesn't have to haul (and waste gas on). Which is one reason it averages 32 mpg.

And the parts you don't buy, you'll never repair. So you can't waste money on that.

Now you know why you can drive a VW for years and years with a lot of parts missing.

And never miss them.

**Volkswagen
Standard-Limousine
DM 4200,– a. W.**

So far, frequent references have been made to the Export, or Deluxe, Beetle, but only passing remarks regarding the base model, which lingered on until it was finally revamped and renamed in December 1964 as the VW 1200A.

Perhaps this is fair, as by 1959 Standard models accounted for no more than 5 per cent of all Beetle sales and the figure was falling (3.4 per cent in 1960). Whereas in 1949 – the year the Deluxe was launched – the differences in the two cars were merely trim related, as the years went by the gap widened, leaving the Standard far behind. Admittedly, for example, when the Beetle acquired a far larger rear window and a new dashboard in August 1957, both models were treated almost the same. Yet real, tangible improvements continued to be exclusive to the Deluxe for many years. It was as late as April 1962 when the Standard lost its cable brakes in favour of hydraulic ones, and August 1964 when its crash box stopped grating. Curiously, although the Standard received the upgrade from a 25 to 30bhp engine at the same time as the Deluxe, it was overlooked at of the next improvement in 1960.

Hallmarks of the Standard were limited, and essentially revolved around dull paint options, acres of bare painted metal both inside and outside the car, and uncompromisingly primitive fitments, such as large wing nuts to hold the front seats to the floor pan. Some markets might have been offered a slightly upgraded pack – for example, in Britain, Standard models came with chromed bumpers and hubcaps – but, when the Australian press reviewed the model as late as 1963, was it really acceptable to be offering a Volkswagen without a glovebox lid?

The firm favourite in 136 countries needs a new factory

In 1964, following the 'blip' year already mentioned, a bumper crop of Beetles emerged – and there were more to come! Nordhoff invested 154.4 million DM in a new Beetle assembly plant at Emden, where production began on December 1, already a few months into the '65 model year. The new factory was specifically aimed at meeting the demands of the US market, where sales had already reached the magic million by the end of 1962. Initially, Emden covered four halls and 140,000 square metres, receiving bodies from the mother factory of Wolfsburg, engines from the home of the Transporter in Hanover, transmissions and frames from the Kassal plant and front axles from the Brunswick factory. 500-plus vehicles rolled off the assembly line each day, directly to Volkswagen's own port and across the waters to America. An archive photograph, portraying a Beetle with a message draped across its bonnet, should be comprehensible to even non-German speakers – 'Der erste VW aus Emden für Übersee' the banner proclaimed!

Introducing the million a year car!

With the number of Beetles ever on the increase, and successive million hurdles appearing ever more rapidly, it was inevitable that the year would come when Volkswagen would produce over a million such cars in a twelve-month period. In September 1965, the ten-millionth Beetle to be manufactured made its debut, so perhaps it is fitting that this was also the year that 1,090,863 cars were produced. Undoubtedly the gods were kind to the director general, for Nordhoff had celebrated his 65th birthday in 1964, thus reaching the traditional age for retirement. Whatever the future held, nobody could take this further achievement away from him, one more pinnacle in the Golden Age. The '65 model year had heralded further significant Beetle developments, with yet another increase in the size of the window glass affecting all areas of the car. Even the slim-line, wing-mounted indicators had been given a chunkier appearance. But there were even bigger plans for the '66 model. A new engine was to be unveiled, offering more power to the Beetle's elbow ...

A world of 136 countries populated by Beetles

Although a great deal of emphasis has been placed on the importance of Beetle exports, particularly to countries like the USA, Volkswagen's subsidiary manufacturing plants and assembling bodies across the continents have received scant mention. While the Transporter also played an important role in some locations, without the Beetle it is hard to imagine Volkswagen's manufacturing success encompassing so many and such distant countries.

One of the most significant manufacturing plants outside Germany centred on Sao Paula, Brazil. Arguably the oldest of them all, interest in the product dated back to 1949, when a Chrysler franchisee started to import Beetles. By 1953, Volkswagen do Brasil had been established, with the clear intention of assembling Beetles from kits supplied by Germany. In 1957, full local manufacture was instigated, initially of 50 per cent local content but rising to 95 per cent in 1959. By 1962, the Beetle had become Brazil's best selling car, leading to the arrival of the 500,000th in July 1967.

Uitenhage, South Africa, on the other hand, could argue a start-up point of 1951, as that was when its first Beetle rolled off the assembly line, comprised of 'bits' supplied by Wolfsburg. In 1956, Volkswagen AG took a controlling share in Volkswagen of South Africa, engendering at the same time steps towards full manufacture. By 1963, 100,000 Beetles had been sold and the car that was rolled out to herald the achievement was entirely South African.

In June 1954, Beetles began to be assembled from kits in Clayton, Australia. By 1959, full manufacture had arrived and by 1961, the Beetle had the second largest share of the Australian market. In 1964, sales peaked at 25,736 for the year.

Mexican links with the Beetle also began in 1954, with kits being assembled at Xalostoc. Full manufacture began when a purpose-built factory at Puebla was completed in 1966. There were 8400 Beetles added to those already on the country's roads in the first twelve months of operations.

Countries assembling Beetles from parts supplied included: Belgium (1954); Ireland (1950); New Zealand (1954); Philippines (1959); Portugal (1964); Uruguay (1961); Venezuela (1963); and Peru (1960). Although Volkswagen did not directly own many of the factories, such operations helped to make the Beetle a truly international car.

After many years 'in the waiting', a Beetle with a larger engine

Some commentators have said that Nordhoff was bitterly opposed to the notion of a larger engine for his beloved Beetle. Indeed, he had once instructed that any proposed Beetle replacement should be fitted with a 1200, rather than a 1500 engine. His reasoning was simple, but not necessarily related to performance. 'If you make a car 50 centimetres longer,' he argued, 'you add 100 kilograms to the weight. That means higher fuel consumption straight away. But most of all you need a bigger engine and that takes you straight into a higher price bracket ...' Of course, with the arrival of the 1300 Beetle in August 1965, there was no increase in body size and weight. Nordhoff's sentiments were expressed in the fifties, at a time when a 30bhp car with a 1200 engine could compete with the products of rival manufacturers. Circumstances had changed by the mid-sixties. The VW 1500 family car range, launched in 1961, had both a bigger body and engine, but nevertheless received an upgrade to 1600 status. To remain competitive, the starter-pack Beetle needed more oomph, pure and simple!

New York trunk roads

Christmas in Mexico City

The VW 1300

Outwardly most distinguishable by a 1300 badge, jauntily angled on its engine lid, the new Beetle of 1966 encompassed the usual catalogue of minor improvements. But the big talking point for journalists and buyers alike was the new engine. The 40bhp, 1285cc unit (compared to 34bhp and 1192cc for the VW 1200) was achieved by 'borrowing' the crankshaft from the VW 1500 and in so doing, lengthening the stroke from 64 to 69mm. The compression ratio was increased from 7:1 to 7.3:1, while maximum brake-horse-power was produced at 4000rpm. The result was a 17.5 per cent increase in power. The top speed of the new engine rose from the VW 1200's 72mph to a healthy 78mph. While that might not have seemed too astonishing to would-be owners of models from other manufacturers, Volkswagen were quick to point out that unlike the also-rans, the maximum was also the cruising speed ...

Six super sales statements about what?

'The bigger, stronger engine makes a difference in performance that is immediately discernable ... there is a noticeable reduction in the amount of 2nd and 3rd gear effort required to get up to cruising speed ... the most notable increase in performance is in acceleration. ... It still oversteers, the power is still marginal on any but the gentlest incline ... but because it retains the established VW virtues of excellent quality control, excellent service, better than average reliability and unexcelled resale value, as well as being fun to drive, we have no hesitation in predicting that it will continue to hold its position of eminence in the economy car field.' *Road and Track*, December 1965

Village in Mexico

This was one of many glowing testimonials to the latest Volkswagen, all of which related their words to performance, acceleration and power ...

On the other hand, the marketing men working for Volkswagen, and charged with promoting the 1300, announced that they would like to 'describe the Volkswagen in enough detail ... to have a yardstick when it comes to comparing other cars in the same price bracket.' Six requirements had to be met, they decided. Curiously, not one of these related to the 1300 power plant. Traditional Volkswagen assets rolled off their collective tongue instead, while in the main a series of photographs told the story of how 'the VW proved itself all over the world'. Clever stuff or not, the carefully arranged lifestyle shots offer a complete Volkswagen social history of the time.

The magical six requirements – and the key to the Beetle's supremacy – were:

Amalfi (Italy)

1. Compact outside, roomy within, with extras at no additional cost.
2. Design and technical concept compatible with 1966 – no problems at high speeds, both easy and cheap to repair.
3. Painstaking workmanship both inside and out – capable of being both parked outside and travelling many thousands of miles, without showing signs of wear and tear.
4. Demonstrably low running costs, using little petrol and oil, even easy on the tyres.
5. A car backed by service as good as the car itself.
6. Above average resale value, no matter its age or miles on the clock.

Stone walls in Ireland

Now the VW 1300 is also available with

Just twelve months after Volkswagen increased the size of the engine in its Deluxe model, it did it again; and what was produced on this occasion has gone down for most as the best ever Beetle. For while the new VW 1500 (not to be confused with the larger Type Three VW 1500!) had enough power to warrant the abandonment of drum brakes in favour of beefier discs, it also retained the vast majority of aesthetical assets of a classic fifties Beetle. What was to come later is in evidence if you flick over a couple of pages and, yes, the change was as necessary as Nordhoff was to the Beetle – but wow, the 1500 as launched was the best! This was a true drivers' car, with real oomph this time and the kind of handling needed to go with it.

Notably more powerful than any Beetle before it, the 1500 developed a modest 44bhp, the key to its success being not in this, but in big gulps of more usable power right across the range, with maximum torque occurring at 2600rpm. The 1300's 69mm stroke was retained, but the bore was enlarged from 77 to 83mm and the compression ratio was increased to 7.5:1. While other models might have benefited from a widened track and some were equipped with a clever equaliser spring (which had the effect of offering assistance to the torsion bars), only the 1500 had 277mm disc brakes.

a 1.5 litre engine and disc brakes up front.

Attempts to tarnish the Golden Age

Inevitably, the Beetle's story tends to be Volkswagen's and vice-versa, much more than it ever could be with the VW 1500 launched in 1961, the 'specialist' Karmann Ghia of 1955 vintage and not even built at Wolfsburg, or even the hugely popular Transporter, very much a post war baby and not a part of the original plan. It is for this very reason that, if an issue arose, it invariably involved the Beetle.

Sadly, for Europe as a whole, recession reared its ugly head as 1966 came to a close. German politicians, looking for a scapegoat to ensure their own survival and re-election prospects, thought in this instance that they had an easy target; an individual who had been a potential thorn in their side for many a year. His kingdom had been producing the same model of car since he came to power in 1948. If only this potentate had followed the way of the US automobile giants, Germany could have easily avoided the worst excesses of the economic upheaval.

Although Nordhoff always declared a lack of interest in politics, as the head of Volkswagen any observations he did make were listened to with interest. On the occasion of the celebrations marking the arrival of the millionth Beetle, Nordhoff had revealed his bitter annoyance with the state of the roads and his surprise that, apparently, there wasn't enough money available to repair them. In his demands for a co-ordinated and long-term plan, Nordhoff offered a 'not inconsiderable sum' to help. His justification was that if the roads were not only fit for their purpose, but also more numerous, he would inevitably be able to further accelerate production to keep up with the ever-increasing demand. More sales, more profitability, more investment. Although it was overshadowed by business acumen, there was still a political undertone.

Speaking in 1962 at the Boston University School, Nordhoff's reservations concerning the Common Market as a third force were clear, as were his commitments to the 'liberal thinking of the USA ... an outstanding example to the world.' Tariffs were low and Nordhoff had every opportunity to sell more cars, but again there was a whiff of politics.

These are just two examples in a series of many, which didn't necessarily endear the director general to the politicians. This politicisation now proved particularly dangerous, as Nordhoff had decidedly different views regarding a solution to Germany's rising fuel prices, higher taxes on mineral oils and increases in insurance premiums (which the government thought essential). Shaking his head, Nordhoff announced that it was intolerable to cut by half the tax deductions for people who commuted to work in their car. Predicting a 30 per cent drop in new Beetle sales in Germany compared to the previous year, he openly and frankly criticised the government's policy, which he felt was to blame. Instead, Nordhoff insisted that all vehicle ownership taxes should be abolished; a move that would stimulate sales and consequently give a powerful boost not only to the automobile industry, but also to all who supplied it with parts and raw materials.

Inevitably, the political backlash was swift and icy. Headed by Finance Minister Franz-Josef Strauss, who had come to power in late 1966, accusations came thick and fast. Too many cars had been produced against a background of too few ideas. 'VW has been asleep' was the banner headline inspired by Strauss in one newspaper, while the Finance Minister accused Nordhoff of, 'hoarding up vast financial reserves over many years'. 'Two glorious initials on the bonnet of the car don't make up for a lack of comfort', boomed Strauss. Challenging total Beetle sales, of which only 30 per cent were accounted for on the home market, Strauss asked what would happen when the rest of the world, particularly the USA, turned its back on the Beetle. That there was no sign of this happening, and that Nordhoff had several strings to his bow, was deemed irrelevant. The man who had been one of the key factors in Germany's post war economic miracle, the individual who

The new VW 1200. The best VW ever made - for the money.

had gone it alone, without any requests for government assistance, the creator of Volkswagen's first Golden Age, was now being 'blamed' for a series of government policies that, with the benefit of hindsight, had helped accelerate the slump.

Whereas Ford and Opel summarily dismissed large numbers of workers as the recession bit hard, Nordhoff tried two other tactics. Short-time working was instigated, but at least some work for all – rather than none at all for some – was more humane. Secondly, Nordhoff brought about

the arrival of the Sparkäfer, or budget Beetle, which saw a revival in the fortunes of the basic 34bhp engine against a backdrop of the old Standard model's attributes at their finest. Acres of bare metal predominated, while any notion of luxury was cast aside. Margins of profit were small, but the 'best VW ever made for the money' did raise sales and keep Volkswagen's virtues in the public eye, while it also helped the company through the depths of the recession. For Nordhoff personally, it allowed him one final opportunity to revive the Golden Age, with an all-new Beetle ...

Volkswagen's introduction in August 1967, of a radically updated Beetle was its answer to criticisms that the prewar design was enormously antiquated and past its sell-by date. Marketed as 'Die neuen Käfer', one simple page of text described the altered appearance of the Beetle beautifully:

Outside: somewhat changed, it's true. But still a Beetle

'The headlights have been moved forward a little and fitted with vertical lenses. They cast a better beam — as you'll soon see. The front and rear hoods have been shortened. So you can still open them even if you do happen to dent your bumpers. And denting your bumpers isn't so easy either. In fact it's quite a feat. They're now much stronger than they used to be. Wider, too. And higher above the ground. The outside door handle. The push-button has disappeared. Now there's a trigger release on the inside of the handle itself. Even less likelihood of the door spring opening on impact. Yet another new feature. Key-operated locks for both doors. And by the way. You no longer need to open the front hood when you want to fill the tank. The filler neck's outside now. Behind a flap.'

A new Beetle
for a changing world
but ...

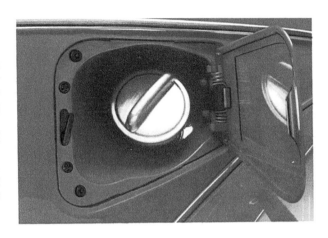

While the Beetle of old had elegant curves, the new car was altogether more aggressive in its stance. It looked chunkier, beefier and, moreover, it complied with latest demands of US safety legislation. After the spiral of depression, the New Beetle bounced right back in there, with a massive 1,186,134 cars produced in 1968. Many more million barriers would tumble, while the greatest record of them all, established by the Ford Model T, was broken in 1972, when the Beetle became the most produced single model of all time. This feat, whatever some might argue thanks to careful massaging of the figures using various combinations of models bearing the same name, remains unchallenged.

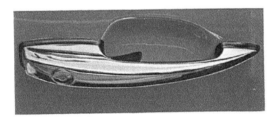

However ... speaking at Wolfsburg to a traditional New Year assembly of dealers and distributors in January 1968, Nordhoff confirmed his complete faith in the Beetle for many years to come. 'You will understand me when I say very emphatically that the star of the Beetle is shining with undiminished brightness and you will see for yourselves every day what vitality there is hidden in this car, which has been pronounced dead more often than all those designs of which hardly a memory remains. I am absolutely sure that our Beetle will be produced for a very long time to come.'

Sadly, less than four months later Heinz Nordhoff was dead and his successor quickly asserted that Wolfsburg would 'never see the 20 million mark' for the Beetle. Kurt Lotz's veiled aim was to turn Volkswagen's back on the Beetle, to unravel the philosphy that had engendered unparalleled success in the mistaken belief that he could do better. The first Golden Age was undoubtedly over for the Beetle and, as would soon become apparent, for Volkswagen itself.

The **W** Transporter

A revolutionary all-purpose vehicle

From the days when owners of ageing early examples of VW's Transporter could hardly give them away, the Splittie as it is usually referred to nowadays has become the enthusiast's most appreciating asset. Just as the vehicle revolutionised the post-war world of the smaller commercial vehicle, so now it has overwhelmed the classic VW scene, with both massive turnouts at general shows being apparent and gatherings designed specifically for it, being crammed to capacity.

Origins of the Transporter

Although Ferdinand Porsche and his team contemplated creating various types of small commercial vehicle, using the platform and as many panels as possible from the KdF-Wagen, due to the intervention of war none of these ideas were pursued. Of the assorted type numbers allocated, the most practical and attractive prototype to appear in the metal was the Type 81. To all extents and purposes, this looked like a KdF-Wagen from the front and appeared similar from the rear to any other van variation on a theme, even today. As for the rest, most

had a striking similarity to a garden shed unceremoniously dumped onto the car, with its rear passenger windows and roof section hacksawed away! While the military version of the KdF-Wagen, the Kübel, was also subjected to the 'hut look', the notion of a larger vehicle with a reasonable carrying capacity only emerged when Porsche was out of the country and the Nazis had been consigned to history.

During the British period in control at Wolfsburg, the officer in charge, Major Ivan Hirst, made use of forklift

Although the work of Bernd Reuters dominated early Transporter sales brochures, use was made of both colour and black and white photography. The model depicted here is the Microbus.

trucks to carry materials and components around the factory. Inevitably the time came when these were required elsewhere, and so the ever-ingenious Hirst 'designed' a flatbed vehicle, based on the Beetle's chassis (variants of this were only withdrawn from service as late as 1994). It was this load carrier, dubbed the Plattenwagen, which triggered a thought in the fertile mind of long-term would-be Beetle importer, the extrovert Dutchman, Ben Pon. Here was a chance to make a fast buck or two – if he was successful in obtaining street-legal certification in the Netherlands. When Pon's application was rejected, he journeyed to Wolfsburg armed with a proposal for a vehicle with a box-shaped body, capable of carrying 750kg. Its engine would be air-cooled and at the rear. Hirst was delighted with what he saw, but his superior officer Colonel Charles Radclyffe – who was in charge of all motor vehicle production in the British zone – reluctantly decided that the many problems associated with Beetle production were more than enough for Wolfsburg to cope with, and turned down Pon's idea.

From idea to reality

With the appointment of Heinz Nordhoff in 1948, Pon presented his ideas once more, and this time received a much more positive response. Nordhoff had for many years been a part of Opel's management structure, and in 1942 had been put in charge of the company's lorry factory in Brandenburg – the largest of its kind in Europe, producing in the region of 4000 vehicles per month. With such a background, Nordhoff recognised something radically different in Pon's sketch. Later, when Nordhoff officially launched the Transporter, he would explain what up to that point had been wrong with commercial vehicles: 'We did not choose to put the engine in the back because we felt morally obliged ... the famous cab over engine gave such horrendous handling characteristics,

that we never even considered it. You can tell by looking at the state of the trees in the British zone, how well the British army lorries, built on this principle, handle on wet roads when they aren't loaded.' Other manufacturers, both in Germany and abroad, had nothing to compare to Pon's proposal and Nordhoff eagerly masterminded the project.

In the autumn of 1948, in liaison with Wolfsburg's technical director, Alfred Haesner, the go-ahead was given for work to commence on the design and development of Volkswagen's first commercial vehicle. Nordhoff demanded fast progress. He was already hard at work with the Beetle, which had to be improved if it was to be suitable for export in significant numbers.

By November 20 1948, the first plans for the Transporter, given the internal number of Type 29, were available. Two versions were offered up: one with a flat and straight cab, the other with a slightly raked front without an overhanging roof. Nordhoff preferred the latter for reasons of aesthetics if nothing else, but following wind-tunnel tests, this version was modified to allow for an even more curved front. In its construction, the prototype was as near pure Beetle as you could get. The Sedan's running gear was utilised and a separate chassis, again borrowed from the Beetle, supported the simplest of box bodies. The only windows were in the cab.

If at first you don't succeed...

Testing of the first prototype was painfully brief. The first outing was on March 11 1949, and it was all over by April 5. Fundamentally, the Beetle chassis wasn't strong enough to withstand the torsional stresses the van body imposed upon it. When weight was placed in the load carrying area, it simply collapsed.

Under pressure (Nordhoff had already decided to market the new vehicle at the start of 1950), Haesner set to work to produce something both stiffer and lighter. The result was a vehicle of unitary construction, outwardly almost identical to its failed predecessor, but inwardly quite different. Two longitudinal box section pieces ran the length of the vehicle and were strengthened by cross-members, creating a frame that supported the outer parts of body. The steel floors in the cab and load area were welded directly to the frame, resulting in a unit that, even when overloaded, was solid, strong and unable to twist.

In order to address the exceptionally sluggish nature of the Transporter, reduction gears were fitted in the rear hubs, similar to those used on the wartime Kübelwagen. Higher ground clearance was also achieved by this measure and the device remained a part of the Transporter's make-up until a new model was launched in the summer of 1967.

Testing of this new version of the Transporter commenced as early as May, with some 7460 miles being covered on the worst roads in Lower Saxony without any serious problems. Despite this comprehensive vote of confidence in the design, the testers wanted to prove the Transporter on a hill on the north curve of the Nürburgring. They were summarily advised that there simply wasn't time.

By August, it had been decided that four vehicles would be presented

to the world by the end of the year: a panel van, a pick-up, a 'special' for use by the public services and a truly revolutionary eight-seat minibus. Following a catalogue of last minute instructions and amendments to the original specification, Nordhoff debuted the Transporter on November 12 1949, advising the gathered press that the vehicle had no name other than the simple term, Type Two Transporter. By February 1950, the first few vehicles were rolling off the assembly line, before an official launch the following month at the Geneva Motor Show.

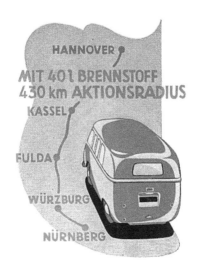

MIT 40 l BRENNSTOFF
430 km AKTIONSRADIUS

HANNOVER
KASSEL
FULDA
WÜRZBURG
NÜRNBERG

AUTOBAHN-
DAUERGESCHWINDIGKEIT

TECHNICAL SPECIFICATION

Engine: . . . . 4-cylinder, horizontally opposed, air-cooled (borrowed from the Beetle)
Valves: . . . . Overhead, central camshaft
Cubic capacity: . . . . .1131cc (until December 1953), then 1192cc
Displacement: . . . . 25bhp DIN at 3300rpm (until December 1953) then
30bhp DIN at 3700rpm
Bore and stroke: . . . . .75mm bore, 64mm stroke
Compression ratio:. 25bhp 5.8:1 30bhp 6.6:1
Carburettor: .Single Solex (26VFI or VFJ to Oct 52, then 28PCI)
Drive: . . . . .Rear wheels
Transmission:. . . . . 4 forward speeds, 1 reverse (without synchromesh until 1953)
Brakes: . . . . Cast iron drums
Tyres: . . . . 5.60 x 16in crossply (initially)
Chassis:. . . . . . . Longitudinal members assisted by horizontal outriggers welded integrally
with the body
Front suspension: . . . . .Transverse torsion bars, telescopic dampers and trailing arms
Rear suspension: . . . . .Transverse torsion bars, swinging half axles, trailing arms
and telescopic dampers
Steering: . . . . Transverse link with unequal length track rods – worm and peg
Overall dimensions: . . . . Length 4280mm, width 1800mm, height 1925mm
Weight (un-laden): . . . . 914kg Delivery Van, 1140 kg Kombi
Maximum speed: 50mph
0-40mph:. . . . . 22.7 secs
Fuel consumption: . . . . .25 to 30mpg

Visit Veloce on the web.
www.veloce.co.uk

WENDEKREISRADIUS

5.5 m

STEIGFÄHIGKEIT

1.GANG 23%
2.GANG 13%
3.GANG 7%
4.GANG 3,5%

BEI VOLLER BELASTUNG

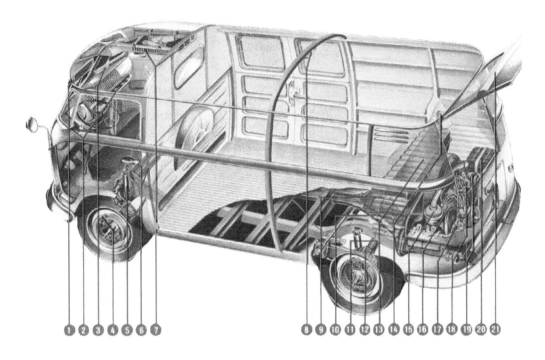

1 2 3 4 5 6 7   8 9 10 11 12 13 14 15 16 17 18 19 20 21

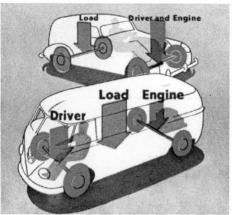

As already suggested, unlike the Beetle, the Transporter was always planned to be a vehicle of near-infinite variety. Inevitably, the first out of Wolfsburg was the Panel Van. In the weeks before the official launch, a few examples came off the assembly line to be road tested by Volkswagen's most illustrious clientele. On March 8 1950, true production began, at a rate of ten Transporters per day. Although the majority of vans were offered finished in the glossy hues of the only paint option available – Dove Blue – some were despatched in primer, ready for personalisation. For the record, in 1950, 2356 Panel vans were finished in Dove Blue, while 1989, or nearly 46 per cent of the total, were daubed in primer alone. The eagle-eyed Volkswagen marketing men had obviously hit the right note when they highlighted the advantages of the Transporter's plain and simple panels as a canvass to promote a business.

'Painted in your firm's colours and shining in its handsome metallic finish, the Volkswagen Delivery Van is excellent publicity for your firm. Its trim modern lines and the slick way it slips through traffic attract the eye of the public. The name of your firm is shown to full advantage on the large flat panels. The sight of the ultra modern Volkswagen shows the public: a Volkswagen owner is on his toes!'

As well as waxing lyrical about this extra reason to buy a VW Transporter, various illustrations ensued, each demonstrating how and why this early form of customising could be effective. Enticers ranged from the simple and successful 'large publicity space' to the frighteningly avant garde artist's impressions of what 'your' van might look like in a very short space of time. The first ever 'advertising' Transporter was manufactured on March 8, and despatched posthaste to the dealers looking after the interests of the 4711 Perfume Company. Soon, this vehicle was resplendent in the company colours and bore the firm's logo and crest on its front

and sides. The more radical paint scheme of the June 1950 Sinalco Transporter lives on, thanks to a full restoration in 2000 and pride of place in Volkswagen's Autostadt Museum. This colourful livery serves to demonstrate that perhaps the marketing artwork wasn't quite so outlandish, and the early fifties not so relatively austere, as many a social historian would have us believe.

In what might be seen as a classic example of full-circle design, the earliest Transporters lacked any form of rear window; not because thieves might deprive a Panel Van

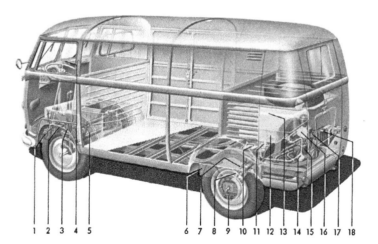

1 Steering gear	7 Rear axle	15 Distributor
2 Brake master cylinder	8 Spur reduction gearing	16 Carburetor
3 Front shock absorber	9 Brake wheel cylinder	17 Generator
4 De-froster vent	10 Gearbox	18 Battery
5 Front axle	13 Fuel tank	
6 Torsion bar mounting	14 Fuel pump	

owner of his worldly goods if they were on view, but purely for reasons of simplicity. Without question, that is what the earliest Transporters stood for: plain, even crude, a no-frills basic look, yet one that encompassed a remarkably advanced concept. Until mid-November 1950, Transporters sported a massive VW symbol where normally a window might have been: a prominent advertisement for the new product.

A distinctive feature of the early (and in this instance, not quite so early) days was what has since been nicknamed the 'barn door' appearance of the engine lid. Theoretically at least, here was a classic example of crude design. Rather than providing a neat cover for the engine, more than half of the Transporter's rear opened, hinged at the top, to reveal the diminutive 25bhp engine, a vertically mounted spare wheel and what seemed to be a health and safety disaster in the making – a petrol tank balanced precariously up and to the left of the engine. Besides that, the barn door appropriately revealed as much space as the average hayloft inside!

Chrome trim was notable by its absence, restricted as it was to the headlamps, rear-light bezels and the door and engine lid handles. Both the hubcaps and the front bumper were painted, while until March 1953 all Transporters lacked any form of rear bumper (it was December of the same year before the Panel Van and its more basic relations were similarly equipped). Inside the cab, which was divided from the load area by a steel panel, was a purely functional

arrangement. The door cards were made of a compressed fibreboard material and rubber mats covered the floor. An uncompromisingly hard two to three-seat bench, single instrument dashboard binnacle and three-spoke steering wheel taken straight from the Standard Model Beetle completed the practical feel. However, Volkswagen did offer quarter lights and cab heating (the latter simple to apply thanks to the air-cooled engine), neither of which was universally standard at the time.

Resisting the temptation to delve into detail, the following pages highlight each member of the model range as it emerged in the fifties, starting with the first available option, the Panel Van.

 The Delivery or Panel Van

'There is no other vehicle like the Volkswagen', proclaimed the copywriters in the earlier brochures produced to promote the Transporter, and of course they were right. 'Take the loading space', they wrote. 'It is easy to load even the bulkiest goods through the spacious double side doors. The large floor is just a few inches above the pavement and it is flat like a table'. Later, the same message was still paramount to the Panel Van's cause, albeit expressed in a slightly different way. 'The spacious van has a floor extending unobstructed from the cab panel right to the engine compartment ... double doors

for loading from the side and a top hinged rear door ... the unobstructed floor and the exceptional accessibility ... ensure speedy loading and unloading'. Volkswagen's underlying story was to become 'that a converted sedan must of necessity have a very restricted loading space and just cannot compare with a vehicle designed as a van from the very beginning'.

Writing in *Commercial Motor* in April 1954, at a time when the Transporter had recently become available as a right-hand drive vehicle, Laurence Cotton was clearly impressed with the 'new' Panel Van. 'In its entirety, the 15cwt van is remarkable both in construction and performance ... if competition is measured by the performance of the Volkswagen the standard is very high.' This was the consensus of opinion both at home in Germany and abroad. If there was a downside to the Panel Van, it was undoubtedly that, thanks to the abundance

of space, overloading was more than possible! 141cu ft of practical space in the main loading area and an additional 21cu ft over the engine bay was more than generous. Cotton took no convincing of the merits of the Volkswagen, when he wrote that, 'it is well geared for rapid local delivery and is economical under all conditions of load or duty.'

In 1950, the Panel Van accounted for a little over 70 per cent of all Transporter production, which stood marginally above 8000 vehicles. By the middle of the decade, totals had inevitably risen, so that in 1955, 49,907 were produced. However, as the number of Transporter variants increased, the Panel Van's share of manufacture inversely decreased, so that in 1955 it stood at 35.2 per cent. By the end of the decade, of the 129,836 Transporters to roll off the assembly lines worldwide, only 34.1 per cent were Panel Vans.

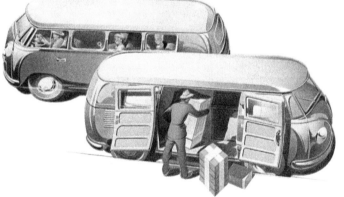

The Kombi made its official debut in June 1951 and was designated the factory product code Type 23. In the imminent race to join the range begun by the Panel Van (Type 21A), it was just beaten to the post by its more upmarket brother, the Microbus – which of course became the Type 22.The first Microbus, built specifically for both exhibition and test purposes, had been carefully crafted by April 15, while the Kombi first emerged on May 13, when one was delivered in primer to a company in Essen.

Versatility is the key word in summarising the attributes of the Kombi. In reality the appropriately named vehicle was ta Panel Van with extra seats that could be removed, and an additional three near-square windows down each of the vehicle's sides, affording light and visibility for all passengers. The division between the cab and the seating, or loading space was reduced in size, so that everyone could openly

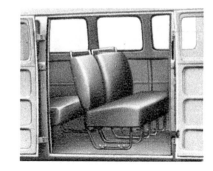

Perfect Kombination

communicate with the driver. Colour-wise, at first, the only option remained Dove Blue, while the trim might best be described as minimalist! Some owners chose to upgrade the specification before purchase, but any optional extras – such as interior panelling, cosy insulation or even a rear window – had to be prepared by the dealers from drawings submitted for the purpose by Wolfsburg. Basic wing nuts were used to keep the removable seats in place and a Kombi, in its raw state, lacked any form of extra trim over and above that of the Panel Van.

Despite this basic look, the Kombi performed well in the sales league chart. Some have seen it as a basic forerunner of the numerous MPVs on the roads today, while even in the fifties this revolutionary model was the inspiration for another phenomenal success story, namely Westfalia's Camping Box. In 1950, its debut year, 1254 Kombis were manufactured

at Wolfsburg. By 1955, that figure had jumped to 11,346, confirming its status as the second most popular variation on the theme after the Panel Van. By 1959, sales had risen to 25,699, which equated to a little over 21 per cent of total production.

For Volkswagen's marketing men, the Kombi offered a golden opportunity to stress versatility, using the best of superlatives. Here's an offering from 1954: 'The seats can be removed in a twinkling to turn the bus into an all-purpose delivery van so easy to load and unload that your employees will say they never put in such a good day's work with so little effort. The six side windows can be easily made into as many travelling show windows for your merchandise. It is extremely effective advertising that costs you nothing ...' A final punch came with the claim that, '[the Kombi] has as many seats as a sightseeing bus!'

While the Kombi was basically a special type of Panel van, the Microbus was in a different league, a difference that was emphasised when it was presented to the world, in the summer of 1951. Gone was any implication that this Volkswagen might double as a delivery vehicle (although curiously, some of the attributes that took it at least partway out of the commercial vehicle sector were scarcely referred to). Apart from an initial reliance on a different one-colour paint choice – to today's eyes, the less than inspirational Stone Grey – a range of factory-fitted options were available. These included a tailgate (remember this was 1950) allocated the 'M' code 053, a walk through 'cab to passenger' area arrangement (M057) and a decidedly upmarket, rotary fresh-air ventilation system in the roof (M055). References to special option 'M' codes, although a catalogue-style detail, are not irrelevant here, as they do serve to illustrate the planned, inbuilt versatility of the Transporter range and act as a taster of what is to come. Undoubtedly the best option of all for sun worshippers was the chance to specify a foldable, cloth sunroof (produced by Golde, just like the Beetle's).

'The Volkswagen Microbus is in reality not a bus, but an oversize passenger car', stated the early

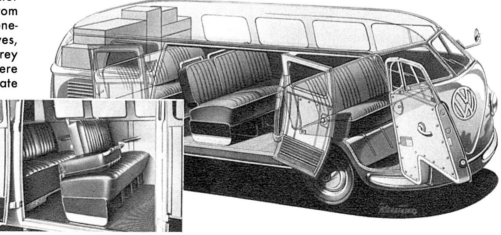

The Microbus

brochures, in what was a radical departure from the norm. 'Every passenger has more head, leg and elbowroom than he needs. There is not another car of its kind so easy to get in and out of as the Volkswagen Microbus and no other in which the passengers are so comfortable seated well between the axles ... The Volkswagen Microbus is a new type of eight-passenger car for

expensive travelling. It will pay for itself in savings before you know it.'

For the USA's *Road and Track* magazine, which reviewed the Microbus in December 1956, it was a 'very good buy with well finished interiors and good detail work'. For Car Life, writing in April 1959, the Microbus offered 'more passenger space at a lower price than any other imported wagon', while

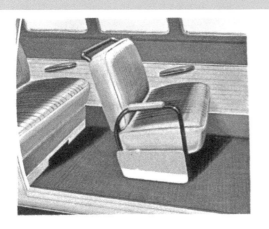

the cab would hold 'three passengers in reasonable comfort. Vision and accessibility of controls are excellent. The centre of the body holds two bench-type seats, each of which is extremely wide and will hold three adults in considerable comfort'.

Never quite as popular as the Kombi, the Microbus accounted for 4086 Transporter units in 1953, compared to 5753 for the cheaper model. By 1958, the gap was still there, although Microbus annual numbers had

increased greatly to 19,499, compared to 21,732 Kombis – an 11 per cent divide. Nordhoff and his team were always looking to improve customer choice, and when it became apparent that prosperity was looming large on the horizon, the director general ordered exactly what modern car moguls do as a matter of course; a deluxe version of the Microbus.

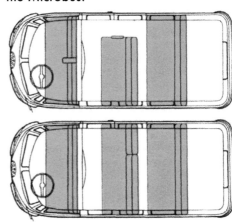

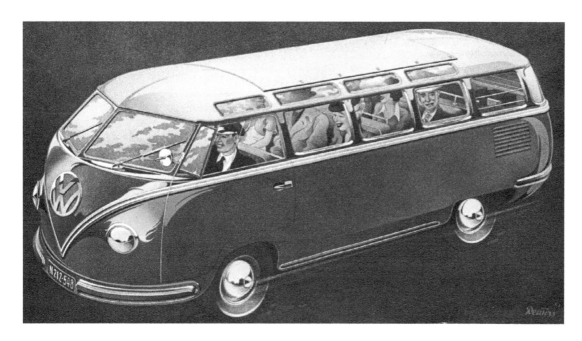

Now fondly referred to as the Samba, Nordhoff's top of the range Transporter could be distinguished by a whole host of extras, compared to its more lowly brothers and sisters. The Sondermodell (special model), or Microbus Deluxe, was launched at the first post war Frankfurt Motor Show, in April 1951. Luxury oozed from its exclusively chromed hubcaps and the equally unique, shiny plated, 315mm, VW roundel on its front. Chunky polished mouldings acted as a border between select two-tone paint combinations, while a light and airy appearance was achieved by the addition of extra glass, starting with a fourth window down each of its sides (the result in that instance was four square windows, instead of the three rectangular ones offered with the other models). As if this wasn't enough, two further windows were added on the rear corners, while eight skylights (four on each side) brought the total number of windows up to 23. Due to their curved shape, both the skylights and the corner windows were made of 4mm Plexiglas, a material similar in nature to

Perspex, borrowed from aeroplane canopies. Fitted with a rear window from its inception, the Microbus Deluxe's was larger than that eventually fitted to other models. From the beginning, the top of the range model was always featured a rear bumper. To complete the catalogue of exterior attributes, the Sondermodell came with a Golde folding sunroof as standard.

The interior of the Microbus Deluxe was equally luxurious and included a wealth of unique features. Although all Transporters would eventually acquire a full-length dashboard, for a few years it was only the Sondermodell that came

equipped with one. With more than a passing resemblance to the dashboard of the Beetle in its split-window days, the Microbus Deluxe included a large mechanical clock, plus there was a convenient blanking panel that, if removed, could house a radio. Piped and fluted upholstery, a full length headlining, grab handles, armrests on the sides, coat hooks and assist straps were more than enough to set the Microbus Deluxe apart, but there was more still. Even the door cards were trimmed in leatherette, while unlike the other models the 'floor' of the rear luggage compartment was carpeted, with chromed rails ensuring the luggage was secure. Innovatively, the backrest of the seat nearest the double opening door was split from its neighbours and could be folded forward, affording easier access for backseat passengers.

Volkswagen's copywriters might have been off the mark when they wrote that 'many leading air lines use this handsome Microbus Deluxe to convey passengers to and from the air port', but otherwise their description accurately evoked the 'mood' of the vehicle. 'No words or pictures can properly convey to you the beauty, comfort and numerous advantages of this remarkable eight-passenger vehicle. You have to see it and drive it yourself to appreciate all its qualities ...'

Sales of the Microbus Deluxe never quite matched those of other models in the range, largely due to the executive price for the executive vehicle! Just 269 were produced in the launch year of 1951, although by 1959, this had increased to a respectable 6241 vehicles; respectable, that is, until compared to the Microbus at nearly 23,000 units!

With the Microbus Deluxe out of the way, Volkswagen could turn to the next variant to set the world alight, the VW Ambulance! Designated as Type 27, the Ambulance, a joint project between the German Ambulance Service and Volkswagen, featured stronger torsion bar springing, stretchers, casualty seats (one of which was portable) and a folding seat. Based loosely on the

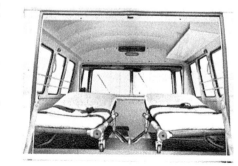

Kombi, the Ambulance differed from the rest of the range in that it had a small engine lid (even in the days of the 'barn door') and a large, bottom hinged tailgate, which of course gave far easier access to the interior. Roller blinds, a buzzer that allowed continual contact between the driver and the patient, an electrically operated fresh-air ventilator and the obligatory flashing blue light were inevitably unique features of this apparently oddest Transporter variant.

What did appear particularly peculiar at first was that the Ambulance was given space and text in the majority of brochures dating from the fifties. Even Bernd Reuters was commissioned to accentuate the Ambulance's lines in his own inimitable style. Would this really generate mass sales?

'Every feature', the brochure stated, 'has been carefully planned to give the patients maximum comfort. Standard equipment for Volkswagen Ambulances includes ... [a list of attributes follows]', making it 'the ideal

means of conveyance for ill or injured persons'. In 1952, 481 ambulances were produced, while by 1955 this had risen to 694 and, as the sixties beckoned, a marginal increase to 710 vehicles had been achieved. Thanks to a degree of patriotism rarely seen today, most countries fought shy of buying a German ambulance when they had at least one homegrown manufacturer available to build what they wanted. So, why did Volkswagen persist in including the Ambulance in its publicity material?

The answer, of course, was that in the VW Ambulance, Volkswagen was able to amply demonstrate the versatility of its Transporter – a feature that was to pay handsome dividends for Nordhoff, as will be seen shortly.

*T*he Volkswagen Pickup had what others did not!

Although the VW Pickup was given the Type Number 26, it was not available to the public before the official VW Ambulance. Efficient cash flow and the accountant's dreaded balance sheet caused the delay; to produce a pickup out of the Transporter required more than the odd amendment to the standard package of a box on wheels. Despite prosperity on the horizon, sufficient funds had to be generated through sales of other models to justify the expenditure.

Before the Pickup could make its debut in August 1952, an expensive re-tooling exercise had to take place. First, there was a new and obviously smaller roof section, while a whole series of additional panels were required to form the truck body. The Pickup offered 45sq ft of loading space over its steel bed, with a further 20sq ft available in a lockable space under the platform. Dry and hidden from prying eyes, this was a real bonus. The platform was fitted with fifteen protective hardwood strips, which helped to reduce the risk of a load slipping, while beefing up the overall

strength of the load area. The hinged side flaps and tailgate ensured that the loading height was both practical and conventional. As the fuel tank in the Panel Van and its cohorts sat above and to the left-hand side of the engine compartment, a tank suitable for a vehicle with an extended flatbed had to be created; one which was both flatter and capable of being housed between the gear box and the neck of the fuel filler, located on the right of the body. Likewise, a home had to be found for the spare wheel, which until then had sat precariously above the engine. A specially formed well was thus created under the driver's seat.

Finally, a tarpaulin that stretched over a series of steel bows was available as an extra cost option. When in place, it not only added to the overall storage space available, but also ensured everything was protected from the worst the elements could throw at Volkswagen's latest product.

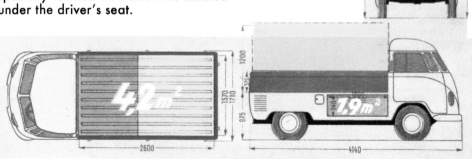

A veritable treasure chest

'Comfort for passengers and in particular, the driver! For he is the one responsible for the goods: driving must be a pleasure to him if he is to move with speed and safety on the road. Is there any more vital requirement than an unobstructed driver's view all round?'

'Whatever the method of loading, the body floor at loading platform level greatly facilitates loading and unloading operations.'

'Any items of a fragile or perishable nature, requiring special protection, are stowed in the "Treasure Chest" located between the axles, the best sprung part of the vehicle. There it is unaffected by dust and dirt and safe from pilferage.'

To say that the Pickup was a good seller would be a massive understatement. From the word go it was a success, with 1606 being produced within just five months of the vehicle's debut year. By 1955, this had escalated to a very healthy 10,138 units, just over 1000 units short of the ever-popular Kombi. A further five years would see it overtake this Volkswagen too, coming second only to the most popular variant of them all, the Panel Van.

It seems as though Volkswagen's marketing men could have sold coals to Newcastle, such was the boost they gave the best selling points of what was, after all, a very basic vehicle...

'Certainly the most striking feature of the Pickup is the existence of two loading floors arranged one above the other – a feature which itself makes the Pickup worth more to its owner than any other vehicle in its class ...'

The Pickup with a 'Doppelkabine'

Today, driving behind one of the many enormous, double cab Japanese trucks that unscrupulous individuals have long acquired for tax purposes alone, it's hard to imagine that it's almost 50 years since Volkswagen created the double cab version of the Pickup, the Pritschenwagen mit Doppelkabine – the final official variant of the Transporter in the fifties. More expensive than any of the basic load-lugging members of the Transporter family, including the Kombi and both the wide bed and wooden platform versions of the Pickup (which had become optional extra cost options in October 1958), the 'Doppelkabine' made its debut one month away from 1959.

Designed primarily for small gangs of workmen, the Double Cab Pickup lacked the marketing men's 'treasure chest' storage area, but this was compensated for to some extent by the space available below the rear bench seat. Just like its older brother, the Double Cab required costly tooling to allow for a new larger roof, additional body panels, a side door for the extended cab section, a reshaped and enlarged cab and a necessarily-reduced loading bed.

Although the Double Cab was more expensive, Volkswagen fans took it to their hearts, particularly so in America, where it was first likened to a car then swiftly recognised as an authentic dual purpose vehicle. Even the rich, if not necessarily famous, jumped on the bandwagon, treating the humble workhorse as something of a fashion accessory.

Volkswagen's brochures handed out the superlatives in one endearing phrase after another. For a start, there was 'room for six people in the two cabins', while you could 'lock away any valuable or delicate goods in the rear cabin'. After all, it wouldn't 'take you a moment to remove the rear bench and the tool chest', which would allow for 'an additional enclosed storage space' where anything valuable would be 'safe from pilferage'. Unquestionably, the Double Cab Pickup was 'a versatile vehicle'.

According to the March 1960 edition of *Motor Life*, 'Germany's latest' was 'truly an all round vehicle ... a versatile workhorse, an adequate sedan and ... excellent transportation for nearly any kind of outdoor vacation.' Full of 'careful detail thought', it combined 'the best features of a pickup and a sedan', resulting in a 'vehicle that is successful in total design'. It even had a 'personality that is peculiarly singular to itself.'

New decade, new stance

As with the Beetle, the dawning of a new decade saw a change of direction in the marketing of the Transporter. By deliberately positioning one of Reuters's finest pieces of artwork next to a photograph nearly fifteen years its junior, the move from elongated, stylised bodies to honesty – albeit enhanced by clever photography – is clearly expressed.

Volkswagen's drive towards integrity started in the US, but unlike the Beetle, the Transporter's marketing path was not a straightforward route to dominance by advertising aces Doyle, Dane Bernbach. Carl Hahn, the then recently appointed Volkswagen chief in the US, had spent a month interviewing various agencies, whose brief it would be to escalate sales in the USA. Having selected DDB to promote the Beetle, he chose Fuller, Smith and Ross, an agency that specialised in industrial advertising, to look after the Transporter. In the first year, DDB was allocated $800,000 of Volkswagen's money, while FSR was assigned just half that amount. Hahn's thinking was that the two agencies would work harder to achieve the best result if they were in competition with one another, resulting in each continually raising their efforts to Volkswagen's overall advantage. While FSR advertisements were more than adequate, the dual agency strategy was soon deemed clumsy rather than clever, and all work was handed over to DDB.

Such was the innovative nature of the new advertisements that the original text remains intact over the next four pages ...

Import voor Nederland

PON's AUTOMOBIELHANDEL N.V.
Amersfoort Telefoon 185 41

VOLKSWAGENWERK AG · WOLFSBURG · DUITSLAND

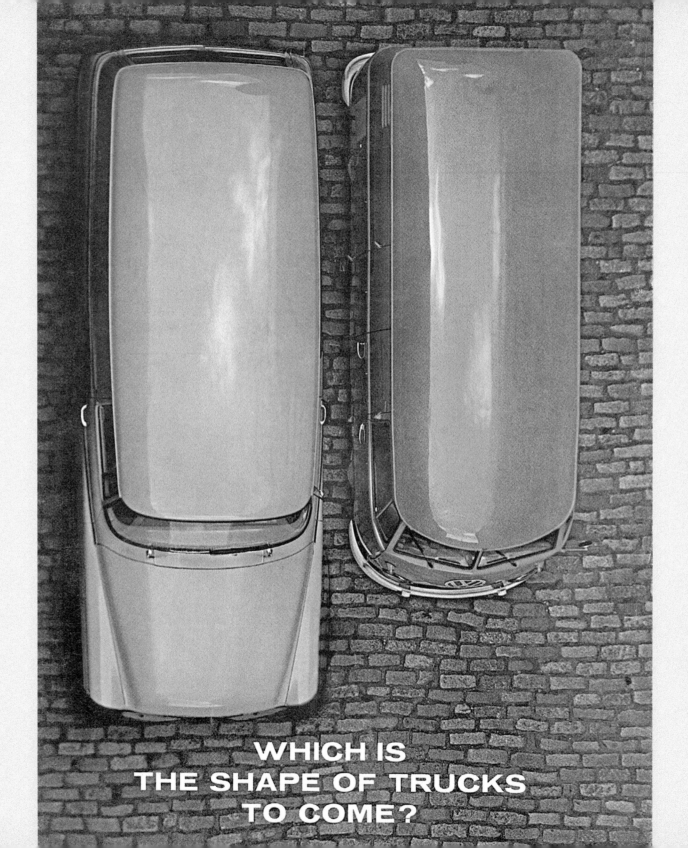

WHICH IS
THE SHAPE OF TRUCKS
TO COME?

You can save enough running a Volkswagen Truck to buy yourself a Volkswagen Sedan

WHAT YOU CAN SAVE AT 20,000 MILES PER YEAR			
Usual Truck		**Volkswagen Truck**	**Savings**
Gallons Gasoline At 8.97 mpg, 2,230 gallons at 27¢	$602.10	At 21.68 mpg, 923 gallons at 27¢—$249.21	$352.89
Tires, 4 at $26.50 each	106.00	none	106.00
Oil, including changes	34.50	11.50	23.00
Maintenance	188.00	133.00	55.00
License	22.50	20.00	2.50
Anti-freeze 5 gal. at 3.25	16.25	none	16.25
Repairs	230.00	110.00	120.00
Totals	$1,199.35	$523.71	$675.64

Savings of $675.64 per year would pay for a VW Sedan (East Coast Port of Entry Cost $1,565) in 27 months and 25 days. Based on actual Case History available on request; ask us for this study.

Start with gasoline costs. Generally, you'll get about twice the mileage you'd get with the usual half-ton truck. And Volkswagen Trucks have 1,830 pounds capacity versus their 1,000 pounds.

And that's only part of it. VW's air-cooled engine needs no oil between changes and no anti-freeze at all. Tires usually last 35,000 miles instead of 20,000. Depreciation and maintenance are much less because of VW's simple design, sturdy construction, and low serv-ice charges. In some states, you even save on insurance and license fees. So, depending on how much you drive, you save enough for a VW Sedan or even a second truck.

Or, if you are already the happy owner of a Volkswagen Sedan, the savings of $675.64 each 20,000 miles on a VW Truck will more than pay for running your VW Sedan. See your authorized VW dealer for detailed operating cost data.

© 1960 VOLKSWAGEN

There are some gaping holes in our theory.

The theory behind the Volkswagen Station Wagon is simple: the box.

Inside the box there is almost twice as much room as there is in a regular wagon.

Now. What kind of dumb theory would give you all that extra room and no extra way of getting to it?

So we punched our theory full of holes. One on the side is 4 feet wide.

(That way, you won't lose your mind trying to angle a rocker around a doorpost.)

And our back door is too big to fit through the back door of a regular wagon.

If you'd like to just sit back and enjoy all

the extra room, there are 21 windows of assorted sizes, and one very large sunroof.

And that can turn a very routine trip to a supermarket into a picnic.

If you measured it, you'd find that there are more holes than theory.

That's the theory.

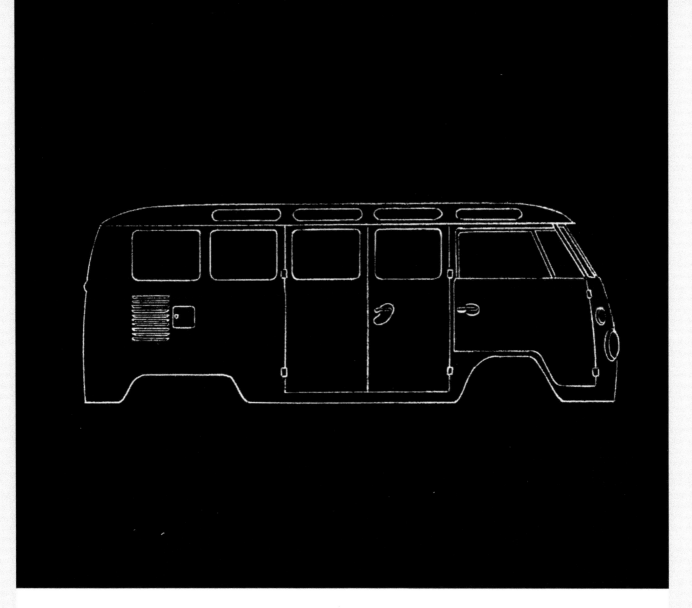

We started with a simple plan.

It all began with the notion that a wagon should hold a lot, and no notion about how it should look.

So when we sat down to design the VW Station Wagon we started by drawing a big box with 170 cubic feet of space.

(Roughly two times the room of an ordinary station wagon.)

This gave us room to seat 9 people comfortably and 13 pieces of luggage.

(13 bags more than you could ever fit into most wagons that hold 9 people.)

Once we got the people in we couldn't just let them sit there in a dark box.

So we cut 21 windows to let the light in, a big hole in the back to put the luggage in, and 4 doors to let the people out.

To make the thing go, we put the air-cooled Volkswagen engine in back.

And what we ended up with is what you see in the picture.

A wagon that holds a lot, parks easily, and doesn't drink much gas.

What could be simpler than that?

The split mind of the statistician

The Transporter story was very different in 1960 compared to the time of its debut, ten years earlier. Apart from the increasing number of variants on offer, plus an innovative development that will conclude the vehicle's tale here, production levels had doubled many times over.

In 1950, 8059 Transporters were produced, an output level that Volkswagen were entirely happy with. The

following year this number had risen to 12,003. Two years later it had more than doubled at 28,417, and by 1955 the total was only just short of 50,000 Transporters per annum. With numbers growing at such a pace, significant production barriers were bound to tumble. On October 9 1954, in what would become the first of many such ceremonies, a suitably garlanded Transporter Panel Van, accompanied by the director general himself, heralded the arrival of the 100,000th vehicle. The most significant year of all for the

including example 500,000, in 1959, 151,218 in 1960 and 168,600 in 1961. The following year saw not only 180,337 Transporters produced, but also heralded the arrival of the millionth vehicle, when on October 2 1962, a Microbus Deluxe was bedecked in flowers and became the focus of a day of speeches and celebrations.

In 1963, there were 189,294 Transporters produced. In 1964, the figure bumped over the 200,000 mark for the first time (albeit by a mere 325 units), while curiously the following year saw a nose dive to 189,876 vehicles (remember that it was in 1965 that the Beetle first bounced past the unbelievable million post in a twelve-month period.) Perhaps rumours were starting to circulate that a revamped van was in the pipeline. Whatever the reason, in 1966, the figure increased to 191,373 and, when everything went pear-shaped in 1967 thanks to the Europe-wide recession, 162,741 Transporters were still produced. What this figure doesn't reveal is how many were Splitties and what proportion belonged to the second-generation van launched in August; what is definite is that the very last Splittie rolled off the assembly line in July 1967 and that 1,833,000 Transporters of this type had been built.

Having galloped through the numbers game, there's a need to backtrack. Not only had the Transporter moved factory in its first decade, it had also undergone a major facelift – a move entirely in keeping with Heinz Nordhoff's policy of continual improvement, which applied to all models under his benevolent wing.

Transporter was probably 1956, as will be explained shortly. There were 62,500 produced, contributing handsomely to Volkswagen's overall profitability and assisting the programme of continual reinvestment.

In 1957, numbers further jumped to 91,993, and in 1958, more Transporters were produced in twelve months than it had previously taken over five years to amass – a magical 105,562 vehicles. From hereon in it was onwards and upwards, with 129,836 rolling off the assembly line,

The Transporter receives a facelift

Comparing the Transporter featured on this and subsequent pages, to the photographs on pages 54 to 57, it's clear even to the inexperienced eye that changes had been made to the vehicle's appearance. Although less noticeable, thanks to the deliberate exaggerations in Reuters's artwork, a difference in look can be detected between the Microbus Deluxe painting on pages 52/53 and the skilful drawing on page 71. Put simply, the reason is that the Transporter was given a face-lift in March 1955.

Most notable was the emergence of a peak on the roof panel at the Transporter's front. Although aesthetically more pleasing, this wasn't a case of Nordhoff pandering to the whims of the stylists. The peak was added for the very practical purpose of improving fresh-air ventilation in the cab. A vent covered with metal gauze was positioned above the division between the two windows that gave the Transporter its Splittie nickname. Air was sucked through the gauze, into a metal collection and distribution box, which was positioned underneath the roof of the cab. A metal handle could be adjusted to allow more or less air to circulate accordingly. The peak made the Transporter appear more homely, a rare feat considering that the van already had what many considered to be a happy smiling face.

At the rear, the 'barn door' was banished to its rightful farmyard home and given a much smaller replacement. Although access to the engine was obviously more restricted, it did allow the design team to incorporate a top opening tailgate above it, which improved both luggage access and the vehicle's general versatility. Inevitably, the spare wheel moved home at the same time, being relocated to the cab, where it sat in a well stamped into the cab's rear wall.

It is worth making brief reference to the replacement

of the barn door's old 'T'-handle, by a locking mechanism operated by a large key. Another Transporter nickname was born, as this was quickly christened the 'church key'.

Inside, the single binnacle pod above the steering wheel was replaced right across the range, with a redesigned version of the Microbus Deluxe's full-width dashboard. This gave the Transporter's interior a more modern, yet still functional appearance. Also out was the three-spoke steering wheel, replaced by a two-spoke version. Of course,

the Microbus Deluxe received at least two upmarket variants on the new theme. A Wolfsburg Crest appeared on the steering wheel horn button, while on the dash, the painted ashtray was chromed for the top of the range model.

Finally in this rapid overview, mention should be made of the reduction in size of the road wheels, from the original 16in monsters to 15in, while the tyres fitted became chunkier 6.40 x15 cross-ply, instead of the relatively skinny 5.50 x16 examples.

In which the Transporter moves home

By the end of 1954, Wolfsburg was carefully and conscientiously producing over 242,000 vehicles a year between the Beetle and the Transporter. While this was by no means near the capacity originally planned by the Nazis, or close to the targets Nordhoff had set himself for Volkswagen as a whole, he was eager to plan ahead, separating car and commercial vehicle production to avoid potential conflict. On January 24 1955, it was decided that a new factory would be built, one away from Wolfsburg – where the pool of available labour was forever dwindling, as the factory consumed more and more workers simply in its attempt to keep pace with demand.

300 mayors made presentations on behalf of their towns, each eager to accommodate Volkswagen. Nordhoff eventually chose Stöcken, a suburb of Hanover, which at some 47 miles distant from the mother plant was sufficiently near to ensure effective communication, but far enough away to draw on a totally separate and eager labour pool, particularly as unemployment in the area

From Wolfsburg to Hanover

stood at just over 20,000. According to those close to Nordhoff, no specific budget had been allocated for the factory, but thanks to his delegation of a loyal lieutenant to oversee the build, all ran smoothly. Construction work started as early as March 1 1955.

At first, a little over 6000 people worked at Hanover, compared to almost 32,000 at Wolfsburg. Production began on March 8 1956, with the first vehicle off the new assembly line being a Pickup finished in Dove Blue. A new railway, linked to the main network,

also first saw service on that same day, delivering an initial four vehicles to the harbour for shipping. Until April 19, or a little over a month, production continued in parallel, before Wolfsburg rightly turned all its attentions to the Beetle. Curiously in some ways, Wolfsburg – not Hanover – had been responsible for the revised Splittie, but from now on, all revamps and additional models would emerge from Volkswagen's dedicated Transporter factory. The sixties would see much evidence of both ...

Boosting sales in the Nordhoff style

On January 5 1960, Nordhoff gathered the Transporter dealers together for a pep talk. 'There simply does not exist any reason why truck sales should be good in one country and poor in a neighbouring country. I know that this isn't an easy business to get, but I repeat what I said two years ago – that the really big period for the Transporter hasn't even arrived yet. He who is smart will take his chances now, to prepare himself. I've asked our sales department for years whether we shouldn't enlarge Hanover's capacity ... I now ask again with increasing urgency, for it takes at least two years to implement such a decision. ... Today, we produce 530 [Transporters] a day and I'm certain that even this isn't enough! ... We must move ahead, not in a wild kind of optimism ... but with the courage to do what has never been tried before, to take what the Americans call a calculated risk'. The hoped for result was a leap in Transporter sales: and Nordhoff made it happen.Throughout the seventeen years of the Transporter's first incarnation, very few adverse comments on it were put into print. It could be argued that this initial reaction was due to the revolutionary nature of the vehicle. But by the sixties, other manufacturers were copying Volkswagen's concept and most journalists appear to have

What the journalists had to say

thought that while imitation might be the sincerest form of flattery, the original was still leaps and bounds ahead of the rest of the bunch. Here are some adulatory reviews from the fifties and sixties...'In spite of a few disbelievers who can't quite see why anyone would actually want to ride around in one of those funny looking things, there seems no doubt that the VV wagon is here to stay. The boldly practical concept is just too good to pass by.' (*Hot Rod Special*, 1963) 'Ever since its introduction in 1955, the Volkswagen ... Kombi has enjoyed constantly increasing popularity. It can carry 10 husky adults ... and 28cu.ft. of luggage. There's so much room inside – youngsters can walk upright in the rear space and there's heaps of headroom for seated six-footers ...' (*Car South Africa*, August 1966)'The Transporter offers everything a vehicle owner or passenger could want' (*Das Automobil*, September 1957)'The greatest in the world would be the only way of describing the Volkswagen Station wagon if there was anything around to compare it with. ... It is the only station wagon I have ever seen that has enough up and down room and forward and aft to take the station with you – if you want to ... For what it is ... it's unquestionably the world's greatest buy.' (*Mechanix*, 1952)

Going up in the world –
The VW High Roofed Delivery Van

The final addition to the mainstream range of Transporter variants was added in the sixties, when Volkswagen had already said farewell to Herr Reuters. Launched in 1961, for the '62 model year, the High Roofed Panel Van featured not unnaturally, an enlarged roof area, which was made entirely out of steel. It also had extended doors and panels, and even included higher positioned louvres, thus ensuring the load compartment was fully ventilated. However, a line had to be drawn somewhere and the tailgate remained the standard size, without affecting the look of Volkswagen's high-flyer. The result of the extensions was that the new addition stood at a lofty 228.5cm from the ground to the top of the roof, compared to 192.5cm for a straightforward Panel Van. The vehicle immediately proved extremely popular with the likes of glaziers, members of the clothing trade and even the large-parcel carrying German post office, who were all delighted that a vehicle had been built specifically to suit their kind of business. Volkswagen's copywriters had no problems in pointing out the High Roofed Panel Van's advantages ...' ... Some companies need a larger load space – because they have to carry bulky or odd shaped objects. We have designed the VW High Roofed Delivery Van especially for this purpose. The vehicle itself is the same – we've only made it taller. ... It has more load space of course. Instead of 170cu. ft., you have 212cu. ft. of space in the load compartment. Goods can be arranged neatly. Plenty of room to work in – means that you can stand up while inside the load compartment.' ... but the following crafty reason for buying the van was quite a deviation from their 'honesty over exaggeration' policy: 'An added feature: greater surface for advertising. Just pay the sign writer and the vehicle will advertise for you wherever it goes at no further expense' The introduction of the High Roofed Delivery Van offered another good prospect to those who wished to customise a Transporter to suit their needs. The ability to stand up in the loading area meant that here was an opportunity to turn it into, for example, a mobile café. The special options which already abounded would now only increase.

Keeping ahead of the Jones's – the power game

Apart from numerous small improvements to the Transporter's make-up taking place at the beginning of each new model year, plus a catalogue of minor amendments occurring at other times, there were a handful of other landmark changes significant enough to warrant description. Following the arrival of the VW 1500 in late 1961, it didn't take all that long for a power connection to be made. Here was an engine with more clout, which could be slotted into the now somewhat underpowered Transporter. As launched, the Transporter simply borrowed the Beetle's power plant and when, at the end of 1953, the car was upgraded from 25 to 30bhp, the Transporter duly followed suit. However, by the end of the decade, the Transporter was ahead in the game, as in May 1959 it had received a totally redesigned 30bhp engine, with few if any interchangeable parts. The goal was efficiency, as demonstrated by stronger crankcase halves, wider spaced cylinders for better engine cooling and a sturdier crankshaft. The cylinders were redesigned, leading to an increase in the compression ratio from 6.1:1 to 6.6:1. Reducing the speed of the cooling fan had the effect of cutting engine noise. A new gearbox, added at the same time, offered synchromesh on all forward gears, instead of just the top three, which had been the case for most of the fifties. Just thirteen months later, the compression ratio was raised once more, on this occasion to 7.0:1, while a new carburettor added to the resultant increase from 30 to 34bhp. Within two months the Beetle had caught up, as in Deluxe form at least it was given the new 34bhp engine. The Transporter leapt ahead of the Beetle once more when the 1500's engine was shoehorned into it, although it retained the range's more conventional fan, cooling trays and dipstick. Initially the 42bhp unit was only available to US customers, but two months later in March 1963 it became an option on all other markets – albeit one that was restricted to the more up-market people carriers. Panel Van and Pickup owners had to wait until the start of the '64 model year before they could opt for the engine that gave a top speed of 65mph and raised the payload to 1000kg. As the majority of would-be Transporter owners opted for the larger engine, the sluggish 34bhp unit was finally removed from the range in the autumn of 1965, a month or two after the Beetle had received its own upgrade to a 1285cc engine.

Modern times

Apart from the hidden changes – the final significant increase in engine size and, for the '67 model year, the banishing of anachronistic 6v electrics – a glance at the characteristics of the Transporters illustrated on pages 82 onwards shows the number of ways in which the vehicle was modified, all of which were in keeping with the spirit of the decade.One long-overdue arrival was the fuel gauge, which made its debut with the 1962 model, in the form of a neat circular VDO fitment. Volkswagen was way behind the times in its reliance on a fuel tap for the Transporter and the Beetle into the sixties.Not including the idiosyncrasies of US models – where legislation demanded upgrades long before they filtered through to the rest of the Volkswagen world – bullet-style indicators on the Transporter's front replaced antiquated semaphores for the '61 model year. Within the relatively short time of three years, the new lenses themselves were changed, this time with an item known by yet another Transporter nickname, the so-called 'fish-eye' lens. At the rear of the vehicle

similar modifications were taking place, so that by the start of the '62 model year, all Transporters had two-section rear lights, clearly identifying to following motorists what a driver intended – providing he remembered to operate the appropriate control! The 1964 model saw one of the most endearing features of the Microbus Deluxe disappear, as all appropriate models were endowed with a much larger rear window, increasing the driver's available field of vision considerably. Sadly, this increase meant that the charming curved corner windows, which had been a hallmark of the Microbus Deluxe from its initial appearance well over a decade earlier, were lost forever. The 23-window model became the 21 and with it, some of the vehicle's appeal was lost. Also in 1964, the Transporter's wheels were reduced from 15 to 14in, an odd move that wasn't passed onto the Beetle and wasn't characteristic of the modern technology associated with Volkswagen's new car for the decade, the VW 1500, or Type 3.

How many variations of the VW Transporter can you account for?

Throughout the pages so far allocated to the Transporter, there has been a message of diversity and flexibility. Perhaps the VW Ambulance, a featured vehicle in the vast majority of literature from the fifties – and presented centrally in the third row of the many options on the cover of this '66 model year brochure – epitomises Volkswagen's passion for its commercial vehicle. From the start the Transporter was envisaged as a vehicle designed to be adapted for any use imaginable. Amongst the rest, the Pickup in both its double cab and widened load-bed version is easy to spot, as are the High Roofed Delivery Van, straightforward Kombis and both Microbuses: the no-frills model and the chrome and window adorned Deluxe version. Apart from the Ambulance, there is a fire truck and what appears to be three examples of the Panel Van painted in the colours of the Deutsche Bundespost.

From VW Ambulance to Panel Van with twin loading doors!

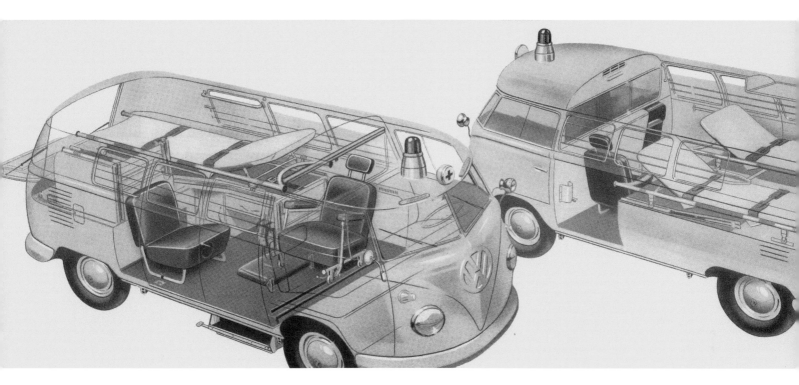

Alongside a Reuters interpretation of the VW Ambulance as it might have looked for the '61 model year, here's a chance to appreciate just how many options were available when ordering a VW Transporter. Apart from variations on specific model themes, there was also an endless list of official factory options, identifiable by their 'M', or Mehrausstattung, codes. Space, and a wish to avoid too much detail, prevents more than a little scratch on the surface of both incredibly long lists ... Panel Vans, Kombis and the basic Microbus could be specified with loading doors on either the left or right sides, or even both if wanted. Two out of the three, the straightforward Panel Van being the exception, could be specified with a sliding roof, while the range-topping

Microbus Deluxe was available to order complete with a straightforward tin top. Both the Kombi and the Panel Van were obtainable as fire trucks, and there was an option for Microbus Deluxe owners to 'walk through' from the cab to the rear seating areas. Double Cab Pickup owners could choose whether the rear passenger door was on the right or the left, while 'ordinary' Pickups could be specified with a locker lid to either the right or left. The Ambulance service might want left-side doors on a left-hand drive vehicle, and if they did, it was catered for.

Having covered some specific themes, turn the page to look through a few 'M' codes.

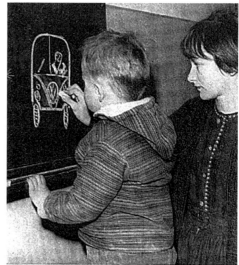

**'M' is for
'Mehrausstatting'
optional equipment
'S' is for school bus**

The abundance of optional extras included something as simple as an Ambulance without a stretcher and as immensely complicated as the VW Breakdown Truck. This option, based on the VW Double Cab Pickup, included items like flashing lights, tow hooks fitted at both the front and the rear, chrome hubcaps and even a fold down desk in the passenger area. Naturally, the package also incorporated sufficient specialist tools to be able to cope with all but the most complex of breakdowns. By comparison, reinforced sides, an extended steel or wooden platform and possibly even a long load extension for the Pickup, and an Eberspächer stationery petrol heater for both it and the Ambulance, seemed small fry by comparison.

Before such things were standard, both a rear window and bumper could be specified, and once these items were the norm you could choose not to have either. The Panel Van might be offered without a cab partition; it could also be specified with a sliding window in the partition to avoid, for example, over-familiar communication between different ranks. It might even arrive complete with a swivelling driver's seat, and it was conceivable that it would have double doors but lack any form of cab partition. An owner might want a rubber mat to cover the load area. He could specify a Kombi or Microbus with a rear seat only, or his preference might be the trimmings of the Microbus Deluxe with a roof panel bereft of both the sliding roof and windows. The inconvenience of doors swinging freely in the wind might be overcome by single, or even double, sliding doors. Before the arrival of the 'peaked cap' roof in 1955, another option was the 'Behr' air-ventilator fan, and those who didn't trust their ability to judge how much fuel was left could specify a speedometer with a fuel gauge. Customers looking for a little of the Microbus Deluxe's luxury could pay a little extra and add a full-width dashboard to the more humble offering in the range. US-style overriders became nearly as popular an addition to certain categories of Transporter as they did on sixties Beetles, while best of all were the so-called 'Safari' windows. These allowed both the driver and front seat passengers to get that fresh-air-in-the-face feeling, as the panes of the split windscreen opened from hinges at their tops.

Volkswagen produced a series of 'special interest' publications to promote the Transporter. The pages reproduced here are taken from 'Our School Bus – Safely to School', the story of how a German school in the early sixties solved the problem of ferrying children from surrounding villages to school and back. From there, the 16 page brochure, packed with full colour and monochrome location shots, widens its scope to include Transporters carrying pupils in Scandinavia, Egypt and Greece, and sympathetic text covering the needs of disabled youngsters across the world.

As if every Transporter wasn't special!

In addition to the VW Ambulance, Volkswagen was also directly responsible for a fire tender, which they designated as the Type 21F. While the eagle-eyed will have noticed that the VW Ambulance was closely aligned to the Kombi, the basic fire tender embraced the panels of the humble Panel Van. It was specially equipped with dry powder and fire fighting equipment, and also incorporated additional lights (including the blue flashing variety), chrome hubcaps, wheels and bumpers which were painted black, catches on the side doors to stop them slamming shut in the wind, an external battery charger socket and white tyre pressure markings above the wheel arches. Some of the captions

from *Sure as Night Follows Day* – a special supplement to VW Transport from which these two pages are taken – told more of the same story.

The German police also made use of the Transporter, most frequently using the Kombi as a base in its activities. Options included a Road Traffic Emergency Vehicle, an office, a mobile forensic laboratory and a special prisoner transport bus complete with two secure cells. By 1961, Volkswagen could list 130 special variations on the Transporter theme and although they differed from the optional equipment – which was routinely 'built-in' at Hanover – the special models were detailed in

'To hand in a flash: it's as if the VW Transporter were tailor-made to accommodate basic fire fighting equipment.'

'Blazing liquids, inflammable gases and electrical equipment cannot be dealt with by water. They yield in the face of the dry powder extinguisher installed and ready to use in the VW Delivery Van.'

'Water and foam compound are mixed in the foam tube and pushed out by compressed air.'

'The fire's out! In a jiffy all the equipment is stowed away once more in the red painted fire truck and back they go to the fire station.'

catalogues and listings available at the dealerships. Apart from outlining every facet of what a particular conversion involved, full details were given of the company authorised by Volkswagen to carry out the work. One-off conversions were encouraged, and anyone who contemplated such a move also had ample opportunity to incorporate as many items of optional equipment to their package as required. Some of the straightforward variations were a mobile shop and the aforementioned police mobile office, plus a Pickup with a hydraulic lifting platform and another with a turntable ladder. The Pickup low loader was a little more bizarre, as was the officially sanctioned long wheelbase

conversion of the Panel Van, produced by the Dutch coach building firm of Kemperink, but surely the most unusual options included an exhibition and display bus, plus ice cream vans, hearses and a frozen food Transporter with chill room. Not forgetting the railway buffs out there, 30 Kombi versions of the Transporter were adapted to run on rails. Built in 1955, they saw regular service until the early seventies, mainly ferrying railway workers around.

Amongst the officially designated specials was a series of numbers allocated to what quickly became one of the most popular forms of Transporter, special or otherwise – those that had been converted to Campers.

Seeds of an outdoor revolution

Johann Knöbel, a blacksmith, was the founder of the company that would eventually produce the first, very basic Volkswagen Camper, which in turn would encourage many others to follow suit. These would generate unimaginable income for many companies, and added revenue for the motor manufacturers whose vehicles became host to such conversions.

Knöbel, based in Rheda-Wiedenbrück, in the state of North Rhine-Westfalia, built his first carriage in 1876. His son registered the name of Westfalia in 1922 and by the thirties the company had become a leading producer of caravans and camping trailers.

Having suffered heavy bomb-damage in the war, Westfalia began to rebuild, feeling sufficiently confident to display its first steel-plate caravan at the Hanover Fair in 1947. Sales were ponderously slow, as the German economy was still in the doldrums. Fortunately there was hope for Westfalia, as one of its more quick-thinking people saw the introduction of VW's Transporter as an ideal way of offering a low-cost alternative to its other products.

Westfalia's Camping Box was introduced in 1951, designed for instalment immediately behind the Transporter's front bench. Two drawers should have been sufficient to hold all the essentials for a weekend away, but just in case, a wooden cabinet complete with roll-down door was also available, to be fitted into the cargo area above the engine. Although not quite like a wardrobe, as the unit wasn't tall enough to allow clothes to hang, this piece of furniture was deemed sufficiently elegant that, when not in use, it might be transferred to the home. The Camping Box also doubled as a bed, thanks to four comfortable cushions, and providing familiarity wasn't a problem, could accommodate three adults. Two children could 'rough it' in the cab. Washing and shaving facilities were available, hanging on the rear of the Transporter's two side doors, while cooking could be done on a petrol or spirit-burning stove.

In 1952 a full-length striped awning was added to the package, while a hinged roof flap could be also be specified, allowing campers to stand up instead of putting strain on their backs. Sales of

the Westfalia Camping Box in Germany could hardly be described as astronomic, but as Volkswagen increased its presence in the USA, the package began to take off. Perhaps the only negative factor was that what had seemed such a remarkably good idea of combining pleasure and work with a camping package that could be installed for the weekend and removed during the week, wasn't necessarily what prosperous Americans wanted. However, by 1958, Westfalia was converting used Transporters into Camping Vans, courtesy of Volkswagen's Van Division. Camping boxes now included a gas stove as standard, while a larger wardrobe catered for the hanging of some garments. As a Westfalia assembly line item, rather than a do-it-yourself installation, there was both a degree of trim along the Transporter's load area sides and an element of insulation. It had taken until now for the 1000th Camping Box to be completed, but soon this was to change, for in 1961 the Transporter made its debut as a true Westfalia Camper.

The Volkswagen Camper
with Westfalia De Luxe equipment

is a kitchen, bedroom and living-room with skylight, curtains, wall-lights and paneled walls. Comforts include: two upholstered benches that convert into a double-bed, beds for 2 children on driver's seat, wardrobe with full-length mirror, plenty of cupboard space, luggage net and outside roof rack. Convenient kitchen washroom cabinet connected to water supply in 23 gal. polyethylene tank under seat. Two folding tables. Cupboard with ice-box, portable chemical toilet and two-ring cooker are extras. Striped awning when stretched along one side of the car forms a porch.

your dealer for catalog, giving full details and measurements.

At last, with the dawning of the sixties, the Transporter made its debut as a true, brand new Camper, based on the Kombi. Reproduced from a 1961 brochure aimed at the US market, the text and illustrations opposite indicate that this was no hastily assembled box – although such items continued to be sold, at least for a time. Apart from the carefully designed and executed interior, complete with colourful curtains, voluminous water tank and exquisitely crafted, fitted units, the Camper was finally fully insulated, ensuring its occupants were kept warm in all but the severest of weather conditions.

Throughout the remaining years of split screen Transporter production and beyond, Westfalia continued to develop the concept, with all amendments fully sanctioned by Volkswagen. In 1964, for example, the Camper could be specified with a polyester folding roof, which was raised on the driver's side, giving both eight feet of interior height and providing additional sleeping room in the form of two hammocks. For the '66 model year, the specification was more luxurious and included both a roof storage area and a refrigerator. Both pop tops and polyester folding roofs were available.

Six months into production of the second generation Transporter, Westfalia was able to celebrate production of the 30,000th Camper. Of this number, 75 per cent had been exported, mainly to the USA.

While the ad men get in on the act ...

'Take a car trip in your own hotel – no more unfulfilled dreams. This is luxury that everyone can afford', was one message sent out by the marketing department, extolling the virtues of Volkswagen's official Camper. US advertising agency DDB went further. It set the following text against a photo of a Camper almost completely obscured by its awning and outdoor equipment: 'Tell the truth. Did you know right off that it was just a Volkswagen Campmobile? Or did you think it was a place to live? It's an easy mistake to make, because the VW Campmobile is really more like a house than a car. There are curtains and screens on the windows, wood panelling on the insulated walls, and wall-to-wall covering on the floor ... Two adults and two kids can sleep in it, eat in it, wash in it and keep their clothes and

A typical glowing review

food in it ... Of course it isn't a house, it's a Volkswagen. With all the things that make a Volkswagen a Volkswagen. But no matter what we say, lots of people go on making the same mistake. We keep on saying it's a Campmobile. And they keep saying it's a place to live.'

'With the sensational boom in motorised campers ... it stands to reason that VW would have such equipment. In fact, they were among the first', wrote the author of the *Hot Rod* 'special' in 1963. Describing the Campmobile as the 'ultimate in outdoor comfort' and 'attractive' in appearance, *Hot Rod* had nothing but praise for the numerous options on offer and proceeded to list every one of them, concluding that they were all aimed at permitting 'the prospective outdoorsman to rough it in even greater comfort'.

From 'Devon' to 'Canterbury', Volkswagen Campers
earn their holidays in the sun

What Moortown **said of itself and others** *wrote of Danbury*

Where Westfalia had led, dozens of other Camper converters followed, none more so than in Britain. Apart from the Devon range and the offerings of Canterbury Industrial Products (which will be discussed in more detail shortly), others included Danbury Conversions of Chelmsford in Essex and Leeds-based Moortown (whose Autohome was based on the Microbus). There was also European Cars Ltd of London's South Kensington and its Slumberwagon (a product again based on the Microbus), Dormobile (the trading name of Martin Walter Ltd), Richard Holdsworth Conversions and also the 'HiTop', courtesy of Caraversions. Most simply bought new vehicles from Volkswagen – usually Kombis but occasionally Microbuses – and set to work.

In 1963, Moortown was advising potential customers that it had been 'associated with the production of motorised caravans'

since 1956 and had gained 'considerable experience' as a result. Its Autohome 'conversion to the Volkswagen' provided 'the perfect vehicle combination. For holiday weekends away, family picnics, or perhaps a group of business associates on an outing, the 'Moortown Autohome' … [is] the ideal vehicle … [affording] a good vantage point for racing or sporting meetings and all special events.'

Motor magazine spent time with a Danbury Multicar in May 1967. Its conclusions were that it made 'a thoroughly practical holiday home, due largely to the wide opening double doors … and an interior design which allows most of the units … to be shifted around to suit the requirements of the user.' Although the writer started off 'feeling rather cramped' in the Multicar, as he 'got the hang of the moveable units', the Camper 'turned out to be quite spacious, even under bad weather conditions.'

107

The Devon 'Caravette' Spaceway Model

Lisburne Garage, of Babbacombe Road in Torquay, launched its Devon range of campers in 1957. Utilising the considerable skills of cabinet-makers J P White, located in nearby Sidmouth, the range was originally based entirely around the Microbus. The cheapest was the Devonette, with prices graduating via the Caravette to the Torvette. All were skilfully designed so that the conversion could be removed and the Microbus's set of seats restored to their original places. The earliest vehicles lacked washing facilities – something remedied by the inclusion of water tanks and basins in 1958 – but overall the general equipment level was excellent, although as none of the range had either an extending or elevated

The Devon 'Torvette' Standard Model

roof, options such as cooking were fairly restricted by space. The Torvette boasted a double rear cupboard, in addition to the Caravette's double bed/ dinette, while curtains all round afforded privacy as well as making the Camper snug and cosy. Formica-topped tables (both a folding and a sliding variety), storage cupboards and a locker, a gas cooker with twin burners built into one of the cupboards and interior lights that ran off the vehicle's battery, completed the most important aspects of the conversions. The most popular choice, the Caravette, cost £897 when launched, although the price crept up as essential extras were added to the standard package.

The Devon 'Torvette' Spaceway Model

The layout and photographs on pages 106 to 111 are taken from a Devon brochure produced in 1966. Page 112 is devoted to the centre spread from a 1967 foldout, covering 'The Canterbury Volkswagen Pitt Open Plan Moto-Caravan'.

Devon's range at this time consisted of five models, three Caravettes and two Torvettes. Two of the Caravettes were based on the Microbus, one without access from the cab and the other with a walkway. The third Caravette was based on the Microbus Deluxe. All three Caravettes

Add two extra bunks and standing headroom

included a side awning as standard and were offered with natural oak fittings and 'fabrics, floor tiles and table tops in a choice of colours'. Prices ranged from £1050 for the cheapest Caravette, to £1289 for the version based on the Microbus Deluxe. The Torvette was based on the Kombi and differed only in either access from the cab, or a lack thereof. The two versions, which also featured natural oak fittings and a choice of fabrics, floor tiles and fittings, ranged in price from £950 to £970. Included in the many optional extras was a portable

toilet unit at £4.19s 6d, a cab hammock bunk at £8.10s 0d and matching 'Duracour' cab seat covers, again at £8.10s 0d. Among the most requested, and often illustrated in the brochure, was the Martin Walter Elevating Roof, priced at £118 0s 0d. All Devon material proudly proclaimed that its work was 'fully approved by Volkswagenwerk, Wolfsburg W. Germany', and that the products were, 'nationally distributed through the Volkswagen organisation in Great Britain'.

Canterbury offered three conversions in 1967, one based on the Kombi, another on the Microbus and the third on a Microbus Deluxe. Prices ranged from £939 for the Kombi to £1248 for the Microbus Deluxe. Extras included an elevating roof and two adult bunks, which could be fitted for £110 as part of the original conversion, or for £115 if added at a later date. Other options listed were a spare wash bowl at 4s 11d, a 'drive on or off' awning tent at £37 and a cab roof rack – for use with the elevating roof – at £10. With a more inspirational copywriter at the helm compared to Devon's, Canterbury proclaimed that owners could 'go anywhere, see everything, free from timetable restrictions and accommodation problems … there's plenty room for all … with your gear neatly stowed away in the ample locker and wardrobe space'. In short, the Canterbury Moto Caravan was a 'second home on wheels all the year round'.

Yes, a place for everything and everything in the right place. Study the pictures on this page and see how everything is near to hand when you want it. From the time you wake to the delights of sizzling bacon and eggs until you heave the last contented sigh as you snuggle down with your bedtime cocoa . . . sheer luxury.

A place for everything...

so that you can *Spread Yourselves!*

Fold-away two ring cooker-griller for indoor and hot day out-door use.

Fitted crockery and cutlery for four optional. (Kombi: two-ring cooker).

Fold-away Drainer-sink (optional on all models.)

FRONT VIEW
"Special" equipment now standard on Micro bus (optional extra on Kombi).

seats 8

so that you can enjoy the scenery without feeling cramped in any way. Relax on the deep foam cushions which have detachable covers in a choice of colours. Ideal for the children too, plenty of room to bounce about without tiring adult passengers—there's space for teddy and the favourite dolls as well.

sleeps 7

Draw the curtains which slide easily on rustproof nylon gliders. In a trice you can make up a variety of sleeping arrangements to suit the needs of your companions. Two children one fore and one aft and two adults in double or twin beds, are the standard equipment at the lower level, whilst the elevating roof provides bunks for two more adults. Yet another berth can be installed whether an elevating roof is fitted or not, the child's stretcher bunk in cab or forelong for an adult.

SLEEPING

BEDS FOR ADULTS

Plan 1   A roomy double bed size 4 ft x 6 ft.
Plan 2   A single bed size 3 ft x 6 ft.
Plan 3   Twin beds 2 ft x 6 ft. (optional additional bed for child or adult).

BEDS FOR CHILDREN

Plan 4   Childrens berths in car and rear.

Everyone has plenty of room to sleep, and will awake completely refreshed.

SEATING ARRANGEMENTS

Plan 1
Eight large seats for adults
six forward facing   six window seats
This is the normal travelling arrangement.

Plan 2
Clear floorspace for the carriage of bulky packages or belongings. So you may load and unload with ease.

Plan 3
Combined seating and floorspace with room for movement or carriage of large items.
The main table can be set up outside for six people so that you can cook and enjoy the company and the good weather.

MORE ROOM STILL
If you prefer more privacy the "Drive-on or off" Awning Tent (Optional extra) is as versatile as the caravan itself. It sleeps up to three adults and can be used as a day room with porch, or for storage whilst you nip off sightseeing, or shopping in private car comfort.

THE EXTRA BEDS (optional) — OR — Forelong bunk for an additional adult.
Child's stretcher bunk in the cab.
NOTE : specify which bunk required.
Twin Beds 2ft. x 6ft.

THE "PITT OPEN PLAN" IS SO VERSATILE

REAR VIEW

Clear Floor Space

Alternative Seating Arrangement.

DINETTE: Normal Travelling Arrangement.

Single Bed 3ft. x 6ft.

Double Bed 4ft. x 6ft.

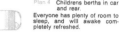

112

The new VW Commercial

Bigger, better and altogether more modern!

Plans to replace the first incarnation of the Transporter had existed since 1964, negating later allegations that when Nordhoff was the 'King' of Volkswagen, future prospects were largely overlooked. A true product of his reign, the new Transporter, launched in August 1967, should have carried the banner of the first Golden Age into the next decade. Sadly, although it outsold its predecessor on a year-by-year basis for several years, the new men at Wolfsburg had other agendas

Although both the wheelbase and the width of the new VW Transporter remained more or less the same, a 160mm increase in length and the resultant extra overhangs of 100mm – at both the front and the rear of the vehicle – led many to write off the much bigger Volkswagen. The real advances were in appearance, with an up-to-date design incorporating large increases in the sizes of the windows, particularly so the 27 per cent larger one-piece front screen, which due to its panoramic wrap-around nature quickly led to the second version of the

Transporter being dubbed the 'Bay'. Gone also were the three or four square side windows, as all people-carrying Transporters now featured three elongated, rectangular sheets of glass. Spacious access to the passenger, or load area, became the norm, thanks to the adoption as standard of a sliding patio-style door, which was 625mm wider than the old hinged ones. Equally significant was the increase in internal space, thanks to a lowered floor – made possible through the adoption of a double-joint rear axle with semi-trailing links. The improvements weren't restricted to visual attributes: the new Transporter was endowed with a larger power plant, due to its adoption of the Volkswagen family car's recently introduced 1600 engine. With 47bhp at 4000rpm to its name, the Bay could cruise all day at 65mph.

Such was the success of all the variants of the original Transporter, that they were carried forward to the new model, although the Microbus Deluxe was renamed as the Clipper 'L'.

K A R M A N N
Ghia

A pinnacle of hand finished excellence

With the death in the early fifties of Wilhelm Karmann at the age of 88, the dream of creating a coach-built vehicle with sporting aspirations could have been lost forever. A first meeting, held in 1950, to discuss just such a venture had ended without result, the primary obstacles being Volkswagen's inability to keep up with demand for the Beetle and its understandable lack of interest in the additional pressures any further project would create. Fortunately, Wilhelm Karmann Jnr. – who inherited the business and became its chief shareholder – was stubbornly persistent and passionate about such a vehicle.

Despite his reservations, Nordhoff allowed Karmann to bombard Wolfsburg with a succession of designs, plans and scale models, but on each occasion Ludwig Boehner (Head of Development) and Dr Karl Feuereisen (Vice President and Head of Sales and Service) rejected the proposal. Each was centred on a stylish cabriolet, the hallmark of the company. Apart from the Beetle, Karmann was successfully producing both a convertible version of the DKW and a Kombi Ford Taunus, each of which sold in reasonable quantities.

Determining the Karmann Ghia

Coupé

Wilhelm Karmann had met the commercial director at Carrozzeria Ghia, Luigi Segre, on various occasions in the past, and now, almost in desperation, he made contact with the Turin-based operation to discuss his project. Segre, while expressing an interest, made no explicit commitment, but secretly decided to go ahead. He ordered a Beetle chassis from Charles LeDouche, the Volkswagen and Chrysler Importer in France, partly to keep his intentions secret from Karmann and undoubtedly because Wolfsburg had always refused to supply a chassis direct when so requested. In October 1953, Segre invited a surprised Karmann to the auto show in Paris to view the new Ghia prototype. Although the vehicle was a coupé, rather than a convertible, Karmann was delighted, and with only a few minor modifications proposed the sporty creation was shipped off to Osnabrück. Nordhoff and Feuereisen were shown the vehicle on November 16, and also liked what they saw, realising the coupé's great potential for Volkswagen. In the negotiations that followed, it was agreed that Karmann would take care of production and Volkswagen would handle both engineering and distribution.

For reasons of space considerations if nothing else, the car was rushed to an early press launch on July 14 1955, while an eager public got its first viewing at the Frankfurt show in September. Priced at 7500DM (compared to the Deluxe Beetle at 4700DM and the more exclusive Cabriolet at 5990DM) it was expensive, but when its make-up was explained the price appeared far more realistic.

KARMANN
Ghia

The Karmann Coupé was expensive to build, demanding many man-hours. As there were no large presses at the Karmann factory, it was a truly hand-built car, with the body consisting of a number of complex panels – for example, the elegant 'nose', which had to be built up from five smaller panels, each welded to the next. In all, the Coupé was composed of dozens of pieces of formed sheet metal, with each body requiring almost 4 metres of welding. Every seam then had to be filled with lead and subsequently finished. That nearly 60 per cent of the 1700 workers employed by Karmann at the time of Coupé's launch were allocated to the bodyshop, shouldn't come as a great surprise.

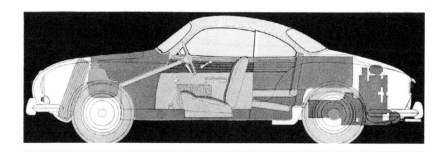

Adaptations required to the prototypes Beetle base were relatively simple and not too costly to implement either. The floor pans had to be widened by 80mm each and reinforcement was necessary for the side members, which were built into place below the doors. The steering column had to be lower than on the Beetle, while the gearlever required shortening due to the lower, sportier seating position. An antiroll bar was added in the form of a 150mm stabiliser, attached to the front suspension, which linked the lower trailing arms. Thanks to the line of the engine lid and rear body, the air filter from the Transporter was adopted and located to the left hand side of the engine. Conveniently for owners, the battery was also located in the engine compartment.

KARMANN Ghia

Throughout its nineteen-year production run, the **Karmann Ghia was more or less** identical to the Beetle, on whose mechanical components it was modelled. Like the Cabriolet, it was always **based on the top of the range** Beetle offering of the day, although at least in the early days it benefited from the occasional extra, such **as a clock from the start** and a fuel gauge from 1957, as part of its standard package.

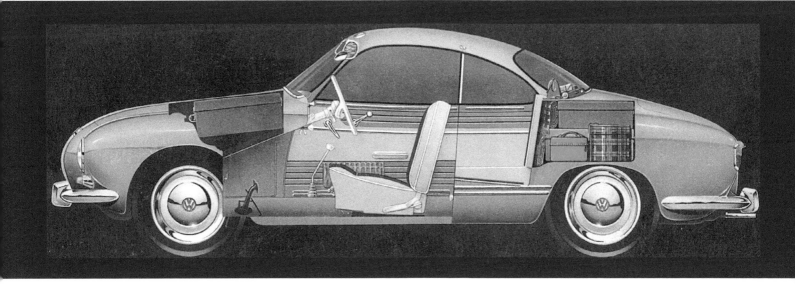

Track	Front 1305mm, rear 1250mm
Un-laden weight	810kg
Dimensions	Length 4140mm, width 1634mm, height 1330mm
Performance	Maximum speed 71mph
	Maximum speed 72.5mph (Autosport – February 1957)
	Maximum speed 76mph (Road and Track – April 1956)
	0-60mph 36.2 secs (Autosport – February 1957)
0-60mph	28.8 secs (Road and Track - April 1956)
Fuel consumption	35.2mpg

With a crop of design innovations coming from its Ghia pedigree, the Coupé was a far more modern car in concept than the Beetle. The doors, at almost a metre wide, were devoid of the standard window frames, while **cable-operated bonnet and** boot locks plus over-centre hinges were a rarity then. Even simple devices like push-button door locks were far from commonplace, and conservative opinion may have frowned on the comparatively high waistline.

The Coupé's characteristic fresh-air intakes hadn't been a feature of the prototype, and contrarily a large number of unattractive louvres at the rear, plus two stylised vents at the sides of the licence plate, were absent on production models. Although Reuters' artwork suggests a particularly pronounced curve on the front wings, from prototype to production the design was amended, primarily to improve headlamp location. Unquestionably, the finished product was one of the most elegant of cars available throughout the fifties and beyond.

The Karmann Ghia Coupe 'Beauty plus sense'

Volkswagen's copywriters had plenty to write about when they introduced the Karmann Ghia Coupé to potential buyers. While clever artwork portrayed the car as ideal for ladies, the initial thrust was one of a combination of quality and good looks, tinged with masculine, 'sporty' asides ...

If Volkswagen could wax lyrical about the Coupé, so too could the automobile press ...

'In spite of its high price in this country, the VW Karmann Ghia is coveted because it is clearly a very stylish car and in most ways it is pleasing and untiring to drive ...'
The Autocar, April 1961

'Imagine it is you seated there ... in your hands the streamlined wheel of this remarkable car ... there's nothing like her. She's the very essence of beauty wedded to common sense. Ghia of Turin styled her, masterfully. Karmann, noted body builder, transformed Ghia's genius of design into a shining reality, superbly. One look. You like her, enormously ... You want her, tremendously. And why not? Nowhere else in the world of automobiles can you find such a happy combination of appearance, performance, riding comfort and operating economy ... Now step back. Gaze upon her ... this Karmann Ghia. Every line says quality, quietly. The easy curvature of the body, the large contoured windows tell a story of great skill in design, in engineering. And a promise of roominess that comes true the minute you step inside, of comfort that delights you, on your very first ride. And what a ride! Sure and steady, she handles with consummate easez ... And inside this luxuriously-fabric-trimmed masterpiece you find cushioned contour seats, sporty seats with a personality all their own ... Just relax and enjoy complete driving pleasure, for brief errands, for hour-long trips.'

'[The Coupé] has an almost universal appeal to the eye. It is, as the French would say, une poupé vivante ... The car's Italian lines are low, beautifully balanced and ornament free ... the interior of the car shows at once the touch of "custom" craftsmanship ... Two large, comfortable "contour" seats are provided for the driver and passenger, and the seating position is far lower than in the Sedan – almost, in fact, like a sports car ...'
Road and Track, *April 1956*

'The new body ... has a purity of line and a perfection of proportion that almost takes one's breath away. This is not only a very lovely car, but it is a new artistic conception ... the Karmann Ghia body is one of the most beautiful ever built. ... This car has an effortless high cruising speed that will wear down the opposition of more powerful vehicles. It is remarkably quiet as regards wind noises ... fast cruising is an effortless and quite economical business. ... This is a car which covers the miles in a most effortless fashion, almost irrespective of road surface ...' Autosport, *February 1957*

'[The Karmann Ghia Coupé] looks better, handles better, outshines the Volkswagen on the road. ... [It] will out-corner the Volkswagen any day of the week and produce less side sway in so doing ... Chrome work has been kept to a strict minimum, but hardly appears to be necessary, such is the beauty of the new Coupé's line ...' Wheels, *April 1957*

KARMANN *Ghia*

August 1957 heralded the start of production of a convertible version of the Karmann Ghia, a model that had been planned since the building of a soft top prototype back in 1954. For press and public alike, the Karmann Ghia Cabriolet made its debut the following month at the Frankfurt Motor Show, where it was greeted with unbounded enthusiasm. Many would suggest that the only reason for the convertible's late appearance, compared to that of the tin top, was that both Volkswagen and particularly Karmann wished to test the waters with the Coupé, before committing to the expensive process of chopping the car's top off.

Previous experience with the Volkswagen Beetle and other makes of car, meant that Karmann hadn't found it necessary to engage the styling expertise of Ghia, particularly as the Cabriolet was identical to the Coupé up to the high waistline The loss of torsional strength with the metal roof removed was countered with a series of braces added to the sills. To keep the extra weight involved to a minimum, the supports were drilled. Additional strengthening was also required towards the rear of the interior where the hood was stowed when down, on the 'A' pillars and on either side of the rear

bench seat. Although the heavier Cabriolet suffered in terms of a top speed shaved by 2mph and thirstier fuel consumption, nobody seemed to mind. Volkswagen on the other hand, was careful to exclude such information from its early publicity material!

Although at the time of its launch the Cabriolet cost 750DM more than the Coupé, at 8250DM this equated to nearly twice the price of a base model Beetle. Conversely, the cheapest Porsche cost 12,600DM, even without the performance to match its looks and price tag. The amicable alliance of Nordhoff's Volkswagen and the Karmann business had its eye set firmly on the blossoming US market.

Like the Cabriolet Beetle's hood before it, the Karmann Ghia's was a masterpiece of fabric technology, well in advance of many other such tops on far more expensive convertibles. One hood took a couple of craftsmen at the Karmann factory at least four hours to construct, while the materials involved were the finest available. Three layers of material were used; the outermost was mohair, while the headlining was of wool cloth similar to that used in the Coupé, with horsehair proving to be effective insulation between the two. Completely waterproof and draught-free, two minor points stopped it being perfect. Firstly, unlike the window of the Beetle Cabriolet, that of the Karmann Ghia was made of plastic, leading to scratching and in old age possible discolouring and cracking. Secondly, in size terms, the window was much smaller than that of the Coupé, restricting visibility when the hood was up.

To raise or lower, the hood was simplicity itself. By turning a knob positioned above the rear-view mirror, the two hooks that secured the hood to the frame surrounding the windscreen were released. The Cabriolet's hood, unlike that of the Beetle, folded neatly behind the rear bench-style seat, affording good visibility for the driver. If there was a downside, it was the consequent restriction of luggage space, already hardly generous unless the rear seat was collapsed.

The Convertible and the Coupé

As you would expect with a product overseen by Heinz Nordhoff, the Karmann Ghia evolved slowly. Reference has already been made to the introduction of a fuel gauge as standard in 1957. At the same time, the indicator switch benefited from a self-cancelling device, while a revised steering wheel design resulted in the addition of a semicircular horn ring.

However, by Volkswagen standards, 1959 proved to be a tumultuous year for the Karmann Ghia. Designed to coincide with the start of the '60 model year in August 1959, the changes corresponded with the addition of right-hand drive versions of both the Coupé and the Cabriolet to the range. Of most significance was the raising of the headlamps by 45mm, coupled with moving them further forward on redesigned wings. Somehow, through this simple act, the car's entire appearance and stance was different. The change had been initiated in order to meet and comply with international standards. While the bumpers had also to be repositioned as a result, of greater visual impact was the enlargement of the air intakes, which became longer,

With Service

closely following the contours of the nose assembly. Previously embellished with just two 'chrome' strips each, a bright-work grille with three horizontal bars now covered the intakes. At the rear, the design of the taillights was modified, making the cluster visibly larger and almost oval in shape. The wheel arches became larger, as did the glass in the frameless doors. To aid ventilation in the Coupé, the rear side windows became hinged, while inside the car was conservatively upgraded. The upper part of the dashboard became padded and the occupants benefited from improved

sound insulation, an upgraded driver's armrest and a passenger side footrest. As if that wasn't enough, a windscreen washer and headlight flasher became standard.

Although more changes were afoot for the '61 model year, with the Karmann Ghia, like the Beetle, gaining the new 34bhp engine (subsequently both acquired the curiously named Saxomat 'automatic' transmission option at extra cost), 1959 was the only year in which the Karmann Ghia was significantly changed in its own right.

For people who can't stand the sight of a Volkswagen.

Some people just can't see a VW.
Even though they admire its attributes, they picture themselves in something fancier.
We sell such a package.
It's called a Karmann Ghia.
The Karmann Ghia is what happened to a Volkswagen when an Italian designer got hold of it.

He didn't design it for mass production, so we wouldn't think of giving it the mass production treatment.
We take time to hand-weld, hand-shape, and hand-smooth the body.
Finally, after 185 men have had a hand in it, the Ghia's body is lowered onto one of those strictly functional chassis.

The kind that comes with VW's big 15-inch wheels, torsion bars, our 4-speed synchro-mesh transmission and that rather famous air-cooled engine.
So that along with its Roman nose and graceful curves, the Ghia has a beauty that is more than skin deep.

Sales of the Karmann Ghia were more than acceptable from day one. While the Coupé had to be launched as early as possible due to the premium on space at the Karmann factory, once in the swing of things, it was quite feasible to hand-finish over 11,500 examples in the first full year of production. In 1957, this figure jumped to in excess of 15,000 Coupés, although the following year witnessed a small drop, no doubt due to the emergence of the exclusive Cabriolet. Up to and including 1962, annual production figures for the Coupé hovered around the late teens of thousands, while in 1963, this figure escalated to just short of 23,000 vehicles. Only in the recession year of 1967 did figures well and truly blip, but again, this was also the case for other manufacturers. In the year of Nordhoff's death over 24,700 Coupés were built.

Although the Cabriolet expectedly never hit the lofty heights achieved by its hardtop sister model, production stayed steady at around the 5000 mark throughout Volkswagen's first Golden Age. US buyers, although frequently tempted by the Coupé,

*SUGGESTED RETAIL PRICE, EAST COAST P.O.E., WHITEWALLS OPTIONAL EXTRA.   SUGGESTED RETAIL PRICE, WEST COAST P.O.E. COUPE $2395, CONVERTIBLE $2595, WHITEWALLS OPTIONAL EXTRA.

What if you put Volkswagen parts in a Karmann Ghia?

They'd fit.

Even if one of the parts was the engine.

Because the engine is a VW engine. And the transmission and chassis are Volkswagen's, too.

Which makes the Ghia one of the best-humored runabouts on the road.

And one of the easiest to service.

(If you're in a strange town, just ask any cop for the nearest Volkswagen dealer.)

But let us tell you about the body. It takes 185 men to make this body.

It was designed by Ghia of Turin but was too sculptured for mass production.

So we farm the Ghia out to one of Europe's finest custom coachworks, Karmann of Osnabrück. Where the body is welded, ground down, filed and sanded —all by hand.

The VW Karmann Ghia comes with bucket seats with backs you can adjust. Acoustical soundproofing like an office. Electric clock. Even a defroster for the rear window.

People accustomed to a little posh usually guess the Ghia's price at around $5,000. Pish posh.

The coupé's only $2,295,* the convertible $2,495.*

were particularly awestruck by the Cabriolet. Naturally, the advertising agency Doyle, Dane Bernbach had a hand in promoting the Karmann Ghia. Again, there is no apology for the retention of DDB's text on this and the previous page.

In September 1961, Nordhoff had two reasons to be pleased – the improvement in the product's sales performance, and the undoubted production efficiency of the two cars. After studying his costs carefully, the benevolent director general passed the savings he was making on to his customers, by lowering his price. At launch the Coupé cost 7500DM – six years later this figure had dropped to 6900DM.

One factor should have hampered Karmann Ghia sales but, despite loud protests from the press and innumerable 'private' attempts to rectify the situation, Volkswagen stuck rigidly to the strategy of providing its 'sporting' model with the humble Beetle engine. Thanks to the Karmann Ghia's appeal, over ten years into the car's lifespan, sales were still not compromised.

You are in a beautiful Volkswagen for two

In 1967, the German magazine *Auto, Motor und Sport* undertook a review of 'sports' cars available on the market. Of Volkswagen's offering it wrote: 'the shape of the VW Karmann Ghia is the only reason it appears in this article. In terms of performance, these cars ... fall far behind the current level of sports car available ... This car proves that German buyers are willing to pay for Italian shapes ...' It could have added, but decided not to, 'whatever the engine's ability'. The magazine was only repeating what had been said on and off since the Coupé's launch twelve years earlier.

While it might be anticipated that a magazine like the USA's *Hot Rod* wouldn't be too complimentary until the Karmann Ghia had been decked out with a few more horses, even the more conservative British publication, *The Autocar* felt bound to say that 'its performance, particularly on the many long gradients, left something to be desired'. And this was as early as July 1957! As for the *Hot Rod* gang, its condemnation in February 1962 was unequivocal. 'The Ghia has clean functional lines that have been a source of admiration for several years. But then the problem of snappy performance crops up. Compared to the average

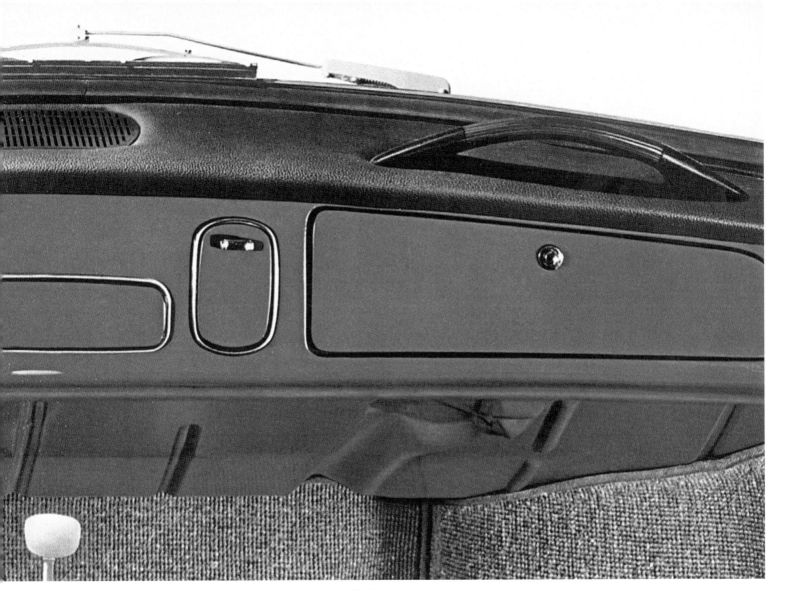

The sporty Karmann Ghia

American car, the aforementioned little jobs just plain won't go the way we'd like them to ...'

In its own highly successful, quirky way even Volkswagen's US advertising agency had something to say about the Karmann Ghia's performance. Under a photograph of the car splattered with gaudy racing stripes, the Doyle, Dane Bernbach heading announced 'You'd lose'. To confirm the apparent point of the message, the script suggested that 'the racy looking car in the picture would have trouble beating a Volkswagen ... A Karmann Ghia isn't really a racing car ... we know a Ghia can't do much at the Sebring road races.'

Of course while there were numerous attempts to endow the Karmann Ghia with go-faster kits, such as Okrasa's special cylinder heads linked to twin carbs, which knocked a good ten seconds off the 0-60mph time, Volkswagen knew exactly what it had in mind with the Karmann Ghia. The car sold well, it was handcrafted like an exclusive sports car. All that was necessary was to offer an engine upgrade when the Beetle got one too! As DDB concluded: 'it can cruise at 72, corner like a sports car and hold the road like one. And it might comfort you to know, you'd be driving the best-made loser on the track.'

With the 1500 cm³ engine and disc brakes up front the VW Karmann Ghia is now even more sporty, even more exclusive.

As with all models in the sixties Volkswagen range, most notably the Beetle on which the 'sporty' offering was always based, the Karmann Ghia was treated to a larger, more powerful engine. The first change came in August 1965, for the '66 model year, when the 1285cc unit made its debut. Despite the increase in power and a top speed of nearly 80mph, Volkswagen thought it unnecessary to upgrade to discs to bring the Ghia to a halt. A year later there was a change of heart, when the 1493cc engine, the legendary 1500, arrived on the scene. Volkswagen sold the story reasonably well by saying that potential purchasers 'already knew what advantages a large capacity engine has: extra power in reserve at all times, extraordinary flexibility, rapid acceleration, a high cruising speed and a long life.' 'You also know', they said, 'why disc brakes are fitted up front: because fast cars need fast brakes'. Perhaps the reality of the situation was a little different. The Karmann Ghia's official top speed was 82mph, while it took 22 seconds to achieve 0-62mph. However, regardless of the marketing spiel, Volkswagen clearly saw a long-term rosy future in its product. Customer-friendly modifications included the introduction of two-speed wipers and safety door-locks, not to mention redesigned contoured front seats with backrests adjustable to three positions, and an increase in the car's rear track.

Nor did it all come to a grinding halt with the '67 model year. For the following year, customers could specify an autostick shift, semiautomatic version of the Karmann Ghia, while at long last 12v electrics became standard, whatever market Volkswagen was dealing with.

VW 1500 Karmann Ghia Coupé
It looks like a luxury car but it's got a down-to-earth price. It's sporty yet it's comfortable and roomy, too. And it's reliable—like all Volkswagens.

VW 1500 Karmann Ghia Convertible
It's just as luxuriously equipped as the coupé. And just as weatherproof. The top is heavily padded and can be opened and closed in a jiffy.

Guaranteed a place in the history of the world's most beautiful cars

Like all other members of Nordhoff's growing air-cooled family, the Karmann Ghia, in both Coupé and Cabriolet form, outlived its principal mentor. Unlike the Beetle, which had undergone such a transformation at the start of the '68 model year, and the Transporter, which had been reincarnated altogether, the Karmann Ghia remained more or less unchanged. In 1969, to the delight of fresh-air lovers, the Cabriolet's hood was fitted with a glass (rather than scratchy plastic) window. Sadly, at a point when – unbeknown to an unsuspecting public – plans were already underway to axe it from the range, the car was modified, producing aspects in the process that were a travesty of the once elegant lines. But this occurred several years after Volkswagen's first Golden Age was over, so it is more sensible to bid farewell to the Karmann Ghia with a brief extract from a review of the brand, compiled in 1982 by *Classic and Sportscar*. 'Much of the success of the Karmann Ghia must be ... [that] it presented a sensible alternative to dowdy looking saloon cars, but was sensible in that it did not have the disadvantages of real sports cars.'

A family car that could only be a Volkswagen

Three fallacies concerning the VW 1500 have been perpetuated. The first simply insists that the car was a comparative failure. The second implies that it was conceived to be a successor to the Beetle and the third suggests it was introduced to prop up faltering demand for a design that was already some 25 years old. All three, originating from a time (after Nordhoff's death) when it was politically expedient to condemn Volkswagen's aims and objectives, have been sufficiently ingrained into the later Volkswagen story that there remains enough credence to make them almost believable.

Few in motoring circles were unaware that Volkswagen was planning the launch of a new model many months before the VW 1500 made its debut. Nordhoff, without direct reference to such a venture, had paved the way for an additional vehicle in the late fifties. In March 1960, he spoke of the investments made by Volkswagen to guarantee that Beetle manufacture was once and for all sufficient to meet demand, ensuring both customer satisfaction and room to manoeuvre. 'We decided two years ago to do something decisive to normalise the relationship. In 1959, we invested 500 million DM and boosted production by

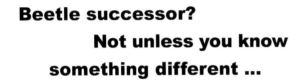

Beetle successor?
Not unless you know
something different ...

1000 Volkswagens to 3000 per day. In 1960, we once again invested ... and by the end of the year we shall produce 4000 Volkswagens daily. Then we believe we shall finally reach a balance between supply and demand.'

With continued economic growth across Europe, typified by Britain's Harold Macmillan and his 'you've never had it so good' slogan, the aspirations of car owners were gathering momentum. Volkswagen's rivals were acting quickly to offer slightly larger saloons at affordable prices. Volkswagen's highly successful one-model policy needed reassessing if the company was to maintain its dominant

position. The new car had to be priced a little higher than the Beetle, but be close enough to what had previously been a unique concept, to ensure that would-be owners traded up rather than looked elsewhere.

Manuel Hinke, for many years in charge of the export department, was the first member of the Volkswagen hierarchy to publicise details of the new car, this occurring some eighteen months before the VW 1500 was officially launched. A year later, photographs of the product began to appear, and in May 1961 the magazine *Auto, Motor und Sport* was in the advantageous position of being able to publish a full preproduction road test. On September 1, the VW 1500 was finally revealed at the International Automobile Show, held in Frankfurt. Planned as a complete range of vehicles, the Sedan (or three section box saloon, soon to be nicknamed the 'notchback') and a Karmann Ghia Coupé were available immediately, while the Variant, or estate, was to follow in January 1962. A convertible was also on view at the show, but without a clear date for its introduction.

Launch material clarified Volkswagen's intentions for the VW 1500; clear statements, which those wishing to twist the facts later should have been referred to. 'Everybody knows the Volkswagen. Now, the new, larger VW 1500 is being introduced. The Volkswagen factory has no intention of replacing the renowned and successful Volkswagen. The VW 1500 is an addition to the product range, resulting from an ever-increasing demand for such a product ...' Beetle production rose by nearly 12 per cent in the year the VW 1500 was launched and by the end of 1961 a very healthy 10,663 examples of the new car had been built.

Dull as ditchwater!

In its launch guise, perhaps the VW 1500 wasn't the most stunning of vehicles. On the other hand, could you really expect something along the graceful lines of the Karmann Ghia for what was intended, after all, as a straightforward family saloon? Some latter-day writers are quick to dismiss the VW 1500, implying that if years later it didn't come up to Volkswagen's own expectations in terms of sales, its appearance was undoubtedly partly responsible. Jerry Sloniger, putting pen to paper at a time when Volkswagen's air-cooled legacy was near its nadir, described the VW 1500 as 'a car which cost as much as those which carried more, faster ...' while its mediocre looks at best might be described as 'unassuming'. More recently, Joachim Kuch was prepared to admit that, compared to other offerings, it 'cut a good figure, even if the outer shape wasn't all that exciting'. Contemporary reviews seemed to endorse this attitude. *Auto, Motor und Sport* suggested that the VW 1500 'wasn't going to upset anybody or get anybody excited', Here in Britain, *The Autocar* concluded that 'Volkswagen [had] not, on the surface anything better to offer than their obvious rivals ...'

Characteristics rather than character?

Although the VW 1500 was 160mm longer than the Beetle, it was compact compared to its competitors. Significantly, it was only available as a two-door model and accommodation for backseat passengers was regarded by critics as restrictive. The author of *The Autocar* review wrote. 'A 6ft person has barely sufficient knee-room unless the front seat is right forward ... nor can he see out of the side windows without stooping ... the cushion of the rear seat is rather firm and high ...'

Like the Beetle, the VW 1500's body was bolted onto a separate floor pan, while its greatest asset was luggage storage space at either end. Both boots were reasonably shaped and sized, the one at the back of the car being created by lowering the height of the air-cooled engine and placing a false floor over it.

Tests showed that the VW 1500 handled well, with the tendency to oversteer being greatly reduced compared to the Beetle. However, *The Autocar* commented that 'directional stability [is] still not a strong point', and 'when cruising moderately fast with any crosswind', the driver had to pay attention to avoid the car 'wandering'.

Although initial manufacture was restricted to just 300 cars per day, Volkswagen took many advance orders. In the first full year of production, 127,324 VW 1500s were produced, compared to 877,014 Beetles and 180,337 Transporters. By 1963, the larger car had virtually caught up with the popular Transporter in the production league. The Variant option

of the VW 1500 proved to be the most versatile and soon took a good proportion of sales.

The least well-known option to see production was the VW 1500 Delivery Van, a Variant lookalike with that vehicle's large carrying area, carefully lined with rubber matting, but lacking the Variant's rear side windows. From May 1962, the Sedan was available with a steel crank-sunroof at extra cost. 'Ideal ventilation for hot summer driving. Good for winter, too. (Just open it a few inches) ... The Sun-Roof Sedan even offers you visibility above', suggested Volkswagen's copywriters.

Just like the Beetle, it was necessary to open the VW 1500's front boot to fill up with petrol. The tank carried a familiar 8.8 gallons. The jack was also located in this area, as was the spare wheel, which was mounted vertically. The front boot offered 6.3cu ft of luggage space.

Volkswagen's original caption serves to clarify how the problem of easily checking oil levels was overcome. '... something unique in automobile construction: oil level checking and topping up without opening the engine compartment. ...'

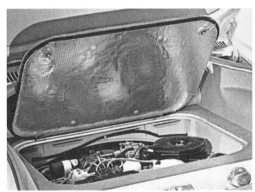

The engine was concealed below the loading area in the Variant and reduced the available space in the Sedan's rear boot to 7cu ft. Within two months of the launch, the engine cover was heat insulated.

An appealing Variant

The Variant was available from February 1962, and quickly became what some have described as the 'most viable' member of the VW 1500 range. The cost of the estate car was only 300DM more than that of the Sedan, which, when launched, was priced at 6400DM (the Deluxe Beetle in comparison cost 4740DM). The VW 1500's 'flat' engine was ideal for an estate, offering 24.7cu ft of storage with the rear seat in position and a 'massive' 42.4cu ft when it was folded down. The copywriters were quick to point out the benefits of the additional front boot, which, while being ideal for storing smaller items out of sight, enabled the driver to 'distribute the weight on the two axles so that the excellent road-holding properties are maintained even when travelling with piles of luggage.' Perhaps key to the Variant's appeal was its appearance, which was certainly more attractive than the rather bland styling of the Sedan. However, the Variant lacked opening rear side windows, while hinged front quarter-lights were optional at extra cost.

139

If the VW 1500's exterior was hardly earth shattering, inside it demonstrated a decidedly more modern approach than the Beetle, which had last been dramatically updated for the '58 model year.

The Autocar was delighted with the VW 1500's 'much tidier fascia' and its 'three dials'. The magazine also commented on the car's 'good visibility' and a lack of the 'shut-in feeling' associated with the Beetle.

Volkswagen was proud of what it was offering. Its copywriters boasted of the 'extras available as standard equipment, extras that can only be obtained in many other cars at additional cost'. These included: Heating and defroster (seven vents), fresh air ventilation system (four vents), front bucket seats, upholstered centre armrest in rear seat, armrests on both sides – front and rear, padded sunvisors and padded dash.

Tech-spec plus

With its tubular backbone frame and reinforced platform, the VW 1500 mirrored the Beetle. All-round independent suspension, with trailing links and torsion bars at the front and a swing axle at the rear, were also typical Volkswagen traits. However, it was possible to remove the engine, gearbox and rear axle in one operation, owing to the introduction of a sub-frame, which, thanks to rubber dampers between it and the body, significantly reduced engine vibration and isolated engine noise. Worm and roller steering, compared to the Beetle's worm and peg system, was another valuable update.

Most significant of all was the redesign of the famous flat-four engine, resulting in a reduction in its height of 16in, leading not only to two boots in the Sedan, but also something that had eluded the Beetle, the introduction of a Variant. Having made the vital step of moving the cooling fan to the crankshaft nose, any problem of shifting enough air at crankshaft revs was solved with a 30-blade fan, set at an angle of 120 degrees. The rest was child's play, as the oil cooler, generator and carburettor were simply rearranged.

In its review *The Autocar* didn't condemn the VW 1500's modest 45bhp, just 11bhp more than those of the Deluxe Beetle. Instead the writer reported that 'in terms of measured performance the improvement is considerable ...' Well spaced gearing offered the VW 1500 a potential of 60mph in third, which, treating top more or less as overdrive, cut acceleration times by a third. While Volkswagen insisted that the car's maximum speed was 78mph, *The Autocar* found that 80mph could easily be exceeded. Longevity was assured, thanks to the typically restricted output.

Specifications
VW 1500 1961-1963

Engine
4-cylinder, 4-stroke, horizontally opposed
Bore and stroke: 83 X69mm
Capacity: 1493cc
Output: 45bhp at 3800rpm
Cooling: By air, fan mounted on crankshaft
Carburettor: Single Solex side draft with automatic choke and accelerator pump
Oil capacity: 4.4imp pints. Changed every 3000 miles
Battery: 6v

Chassis
Frame: Centre tube frame, with frame head at front and reinforced platform, bolted to the body, sub-frame at the rear
Suspension: Independent on all four wheels
Wheels: Steel discs, tyres 6.00 x 15in
Steering: Worm and roller, 2.8 turns of steering wheel from lock to lock
Brakes: Drums all round. Handbrake acts on rear wheels by cable

Dimensions and weights
Wheelbase: 94.5in
Overall length: 166.3in
Overall width: 63.2in
Overall height un-laden: 58.1in

Performance
Maximum and cruising speed: 78mph
Acceleration: 0-50mph 15secs, 0-60mph 20.7 secs (*The Autocar*)
Fuel consumption: 27.9mpg on test of 559 miles (*The Autocar*)

Capacities
Tank: 8.8 gallons, filler neck in front boot.
Engine: 4.4 pints, filler neck under rear boot lid – dipstick under rear hood, outside engine compartment.

Maintenance
Engine oil change and service every 3000 miles
Gearbox oil change every 15000 miles.

Price fixed, brochures printed, launch debut – what next?

Like the Sedan, the Variant and the Karmann Ghia Coupé, the VW 1500 Convertible was launched at the Frankfurt International Automobile Show in September. Unlike the Sedan and the Coupé, but as with the Variant, Volkswagen wasn't quite ready to go into series production. An exclusive brochure had been printed in a variety of languages, and the price had been set at 8200DM, but in this instance, there was a technical hitch – and an important one at that!

Quite simply, the Convertible prototypes exhibited a fundamental lack of torsional stiffness. Volkswagen had entrusted what almost amounted to its in-house coachbuilders, Karmann, with the project of chopping the top off the VW 1500. It certainly hadn't envisaged that a bevy of engineers would be unable to solve the problem of rigidity. Or was it as simple as that?

Volkswagen's marketing team, ever upbeat and positive, praised the Convertible as a 'sporty, elegant car, bound to be among the elite in its class.' Warming to the subject, they confirmed that 'style and luxury' were 'combined with the economy, ruggedness and reliability of the VW 1500 Sedan. On sunny days, the top folds down quickly and smoothly ...', (perhaps they could have added that in such a position it was far less obtrusive than the hood of the Beetle Cabriolet!). 'With side windows fully lowered, the matchless body styling offers the utmost in driving pleasure. Or with the hood up, a well padded, completely sealed protection against wind and weather. The curved windscreen, made of safety glass, is a unique feature for convertibles ...' Wonderful words, but the public, when presented with

the product in the metal at the show, weren't convinced. Reactions varied from lukewarm to decidedly cool.

If, in reality, the Sedan's styling appeared bland, the Convertible naturally followed suit, and while potential buyers accepted that a family car needn't necessarily set the earth on fire, the same could not be said of a convertible. Perhaps more should have been expected in terms of styling, and possibly more caution exercised when, thanks to Karmann's conservative approach, it had been possible to use all the standard panels from the Sedan below the waistline.

Undoubtedly, the issue of torsional stiffness could have been resolved at a price, but when the public voted with its feet, it hardly seemed worthwhile. Surprisingly, the Convertible lingered on in some publications – a Volkswagen model range brochure dated January 1963 being a prime example.

As a footnote to the tale of the VW 1500 Convertible – collectors particularly seek brochures covering 'the model that never was', with examples changing hands at prices more often associated with some of the very early examples of Reuters' artwork.

VW 1500 – fun with figures

The VW 1500 continued until the end of July 1963, a period of less than two years, in more or less the same format as it was launched. Perhaps it was this that first laid claim to the rumours of failure, something previously unheard of in Volkswagen's empire. However, those with an understanding of the Nordhoff era would appreciate that a revised model was entirely consistent with his policy of continual improvement. Certainly, nobody so much as blinked when the sunroof model of the Beetle was updated at the same time, while the addition of a larger engine for the Transporter was welcomed with open arms when it started to filter through from January 1963.

Some production figures have already been quoted, and although studying all the years up to Nordhoff's death might appear to pre-empt the VW 1500's unfolding story, it serves the purpose of subduing – if not necessarily silencing – the sceptics. In 1963, 181,809 VW 1500s were produced, an increase of 42.8 per cent over the first full year of manufacture. The pattern repeated itself in 1964, with a further increase of 44 per cent and 262,000 cars. For the first time, the figure for twelve months of VW 1500 assembly exceeded that of the Transporter. The following year saw a virtually level production figure for the VW 1500, while the Transporter took a gentle tumble. Total Beetle production during that year exceeded the magic million for the first time, making both the Transporter and larger saloon figures look paltry by comparison. The figures for 1966 show a leap to 311,701, while the Beetle fell by over 10,000 cars. In 1967, a year of Europe-wide recession and hardship, over 100,000 units fell from the model's total and even more for the Beetle. So, while the VW 1500 and its variants might represent less than a quarter of what was unquestionably the world's most popular car, there was a definite pattern of growth for Nordhoff's larger family car, a vehicle that fared well against most offerings from other manufacturers and did considerably better than some others.

Opel, for example, with the frequently revitalised Olympia, sold 1.5 million cars in a little over six years, compared to Volkswagen's total of 1.35 million over a similar span. Austin's A55 and A60 Cambridge managed under 500,000 in a ten year period, while the Ford Taunus (1698cc) produced 2.5 million cars, but took over 22 years to do it. Now say that the VW 1500 was a failure!

How does the Volkswagen 1500 look? Beautiful and elegant!

In August 1963, for the '64 model year, the original VW 1500 was dubbed the 'N', or base model, while in price terms it fell by over 400DM to 5900DM for the Sedan, with a similar reduction for a 'utilitarian' version of the Variant. For such a budget price, painted window frames replaced chrome, while the rear side windows no longer popped out. Items such as bumper overriders, side and rear centre armrests, parking lights, sill trims and clock, to name but a few, were dropped.

The one model just like the other

This apparently Draconian move had been triggered by the introduction of a more powerful version of the VW 1500, complete with twin carburettors, something independent tuners had been unable to squeeze into the engine compartments of earlier models, but which Volkswagen solved by angling intake passages. The new model offered owners 54bhp at 4200rpm, lifting the top speed – according to a conservative Volkswagen – to 85mph and a 0-60mph time of 21 seconds. However, one German magazine thrashed its test car, comfortably achieving the same in less than 19 seconds.

Why do families like the VW Variant S?

Apart from the 'two downdraft carburettors with individual automatic chokes', the VW 1500S featured all of the trim attributes the 'N' had lost, plus one or two additional upgrades. A chrome handle on the front boot, a new indicator design, revised parking lights and redesigned indicators were among the most practical benefits of the 1500S, although side trim and wheel embellishers made the car look more elegant. The offer was one of 'comfort, quality and safety', with an emphasis placed on items like the front seats and their ergonomic correctness, with

Because it is so roomy – a car that is beautiful and elegant

the ability to move 'seven times fore and aft', while the backrest could be adjusted to 'seven different angles'. There were '49 seating possibilities in all!' proclaimed Volkswagen's copywriter. Two whole pages of one brochure were allocated to the 'skilful' use of interior space; another double-page spread highlighted both the design and safety aspects of the 'instrument panel'. However, while Volkswagen didn't sell the VW 1500S first and foremost as a powerful and sporty car (for in reality it wasn't that anyway), sections of the motoring press had other ideas.

'Undoubtedly the best car yet from Wolfsburg ...'

When *The Autocar* reviewed the new VW 1500S model a few months after its debut, its conclusions were glowing. Apart from giving it the 'best car' accolade, the report writer was happy to state categorically that, 'there is no doubt about its future success in world markets'. In some ways, the German magazine *Auto, Motor und Sport* went further, suggesting a whole new customer base had been opened up. 'What VW drivers have been dreaming of ... has become reality for the VW 1500 in just two years. There's now a sporty version.' Perhaps *The Autocar* was more realistic when it revealed that 'with a following wind and slight down grade', it 'could exceed 90mph on a few occasions ...' However, what impressed the writer most was 'an appreciable increase in liveliness of the car ...' and 'more important ...test figures confirm and even better Volkswagen's own claimed acceleration times ...'.

Introducing the 1600TL fastback

For the '66 model year, Volkswagen introduced a totally restyled version of its family car and, as it was blessed with a larger engine, renamed the vehicle as the VW 1600TL. The copywriter's text serves more than adequately to highlight why the car proved popular from the start, but also explains the stance that the company had decided to take with what might so easily have become an outdated and staid product.

'The elegant car with the sporty fastback. The most striking exterior feature of the new VW 1600TL is its fastback rear which really sets it apart from other cars. But did we design the car like this merely because it looks elegant? And eye-catching? And sporty? Definitely not. That would flout the fundamental rule which governs the way the Volkswagenwerk builds cars. Volkswagens must, above all, be designed and built with a purpose in mind. And the VW 1600TL's fastback design has three very practical advantages. The sweptback top makes a lot of room – room for an extra large parcel shelf under the wide, deep, sloping rear window, room for a deep spacious luggage compartment and room for a powerful engine. The VW 1600TL is for all those people who would like to drive a larger, more powerful car but who don't want to miss all the VW advantages.'

Diversity of range

In order to clarify just where the new VW 1600TL fitted into the range, it's necessary to find out what happened to other models. The TL or 'tourenlimousine' (touring sedan) was intended as a direct replacement for the VW 1500S. The German magazine *Auto, Motor und Sport* even went so far as to say that 'with the VW 1600TL, Volkswagen admitted that they had made a mistake. The mistake was the body of the VW 1500'. Certainly some appreciative whispers were made about the VW 1600TL being a poor man's Porsche. It was definitely far easier to miss the slimmer TL in a traffic jam than it was to overlook the Sedan, but any suggestion that the fastback was intended to replace the 'notchback' as a breed is erroneous.

Perhaps Volkswagen's literature at the time of the launch of the VW 1600TL helped to perpetuate the rumour that the Sedan was no more. It would be hard to find a brochure that included the notchback, although the Variant was given almost equal prominence to that afforded the TL.

The Sedan gained the larger engine of the new TL and became the VW 1600L in August 1966. The base model, originally known as the VW 1500N, turned into the VW 1500A for the '66 model year, but the big news for followers of more Spartan Volkswagens was that one year later, the VW 1500A was replaced by the VW 1600A, introducing the larger engine at all levels. There was a catch however, as the 'A' version only had one carburettor and, as a consequence, output stayed at 45bhp.

The Variant remained a key part of the larger Volkswagen range and, as previously, included an option for an increased payload, while the appearance of an automatic VW 1600 in August 1967 further complicated the model line-up.

VW 1600
With more power behind it

As the twin carburettor VW 1600 was a more powerful beast, Volkswagen sensibly decided to add disc brakes up front. 'A fast car needs fast-acting brakes', it said. 'Disc brakes on the front wheels and large, well-cooled drum brakes on the rear wheels means you've got the sporty 1600TL under control under any situation'. Whether you could see in the dark accelerating your way out of trouble is questionable, as until August 1966, 6v electrics remained intact.

Although the new 1584cc engine produced exactly the same output as its predecessor, at 54bhp it had at least two distinct advantages. Firstly, it was more powerful at lower rev ranges, making it ideal in urban driving where traffic levels were inevitably on the increase. Secondly, the VW 1600 was more economical, as it ran on normal fuel rather than the 'super' grade required by the VW 1500S. Volkswagen announced a maximum and cruising speed of 84mph and, 'according to German standards', fuel consumption of 34mpg. In marketing spiel this was translated as: 'it's a low revving engine. That means less wear and tear and a longer life. It's got twin carburettors. To make it even faster and give it extra zip. Yet, because it's a robust engine it thrives on regular fuel ...'.

Looking forward to a healthy future?

When control finally slipped out of Heinz Nordhoff's reluctant hands as he succumbed to illness, most would agree that, as with the Beetle, his aim was to maintain the VW 1600 as an integral part of the Volkswagen range. That an even larger family saloon and variant in the same air-cooled mould was not far from production should have been evidence enough, but if more was required, then it existed in the further exciting model developments around the time of Nordhoff's demise.

In August 1967, Volkswagen added an automatic version of the VW 1600 to the range (see across). Primarily designed for the US market, where its appearance was greatly appreciated, the automatic did come with a fuel penalty but benefited from an exceptionally good match of power curve with the ratios and the smoothest of 'gear' changes. A double joint, rear axle gave superior handling as well.

Also with effect from the start of the '68 model year, US-bound models came with Bosch fuel injection, which not only reduced emissions considerably but also resulted in better fuel economy. Of marginal benefit, a fuel-injected model could also achieve 0-60mph in slightly less time. The sequential fuel-injected option became available in May 1968 in Germany and double joint rear axles for all models arrived for the '69 model year.

Detractors at the heart of Volkswagen in the late sixties and early seventies, only too eager to blame present shortcomings on the decisions of the past, were happy to point a finger at the VW 1600 as 'old hat'. Production in 1966, a year that would end with Europe tumbling into recession, stood at 311,701 cars, or 28 per cent of that of the Beetle. The following year that dropped to 22 per cent of Beetle levels, but both were hit by the economic situation. In 1968, the Beetle bounced back and VW 1600 levels rose by some 43,000 units too. However, this represented just less than 21 per cent of the smaller car's production. Was the VW 1600 tailing away and was it wrong to judge it against the Beetle? Knowing that Kurt Lotz, Nordhoff's successor, was eager to be rid of the Beetle, it be right to use that car as a gauge of performance. If so, a climb to 22 per cent in 1969 and 23 per cent the following year might be deemed acceptable. Reality, however, was a little different. The Golden Age of a larger air-cooled family vehicle was over on the day that Nordhoff died, and any improvements made as the sixties gave way to the seventies were strictly viewed as stopgap measures.

After the years covered here, the most significant improvements made to the VW 1600 came with the '70 model year. The front of the car was extended by some 120mm, and at the back larger taillights were installed. All models in the VW 1600 range also received the box-shaped bumpers that had first appeared on the Beetle back in August 1967, substantially altering its visual appearance.

Without doubt, the '68 model year signified the arrival of clutchless driving. If the Beetle became a semiautomatic, then the VW 1600 was more still. Volkswagen boasted that the finished result was only achieved 'after many years of development and testing', producing photographic evidence of its good deeds. A 'transmission test stand' examined items such as the shift mechanism. 'Fatigue test stands' could look at things like the kickdown mechanism, simulating 'the sort of start associated with screeching tyres and flying gravel'. A 'control valve test stand' was devised to analyse the hydraulic 'brain'... 'That is to say tests were carried out to see that the control commands fed in at various speeds, degrees of engine load and vehicle speeds, were carried out precisely'. The result of the years of work was indeed a delightful unit that, in many instances, has stood the test of time exceptionally well. With the auto box launched and tested by the motoring press, Volkswagen copywriters could state that 'the automatic transmission in the VW 1600 is a gem – deserves praising to the skies. And we're not just blowing our own trumpet. But simply quoting the trade press.'

VW 1500

KARMANN
Ghia

Razor sharp design or on the edge?

An integral part of the VW 1500 family

Today, all but the keenest enthusiast would probably take some convincing that there were two Karmann Ghia models available in the sixties. The 'newer' incarnation soon acquired the nickname of 'razor-edge', thanks to its angular styling, and of all the air-cooled models launched in Nordhoff's lifetime, this was the one which failed to meet both Volkswagen's and Karmann's expectations – plus the public's imagination.

Unlike the Karmann Ghia based on the Beetle, which was certainly not a part of the range conceived by Porsche or the post war management, the second Karmann Ghia was an integral part of the Type 3, or VW 1500, range. Internally known as the Type 34, the logic was that the Karmann Ghia was the fourth variation in the range, falling after the Sedan, Convertible and Variant. As we know, the Variant wasn't immediately available after its debut at the Frankfurt show in September 1961, but the VW Karmann Ghia 1500 certainly was. What isn't well known is that a soft top version of the new 'sports' car was also on show. However, like the convertible version of the VW 1500 Sedan, the car never made production, despite seventeen attempted prototypes being constructed between 1961 and 1963. Sadly, structural rigidity just could not be guaranteed when the car's roof was hacked off. Two of these soft top models have survived, one being resident at Karmann's own museum, while the other is in the hands of a private collector. Almost as rare today are examples of the brochures produced to promote the convertible.

Inevitably, the price for the 'big' Karmann Ghia was relatively hefty. The Coupé was launched at 8750DM and the Cabriolet at 9500DM. Compared to the 'original' Coupé at 6900DM, this equated to a 27 per cent levy on the most elegant car that Volkswagen had been associated with to date, while making it more than double the price of a Standard model Beetle.

The Karmann Ghia 1500 was designed by the Turin studio, as the original Coupé had been. However, the contrast between the two couldn't have been greater. Starkly aggressive in stance, the new car was distinctively different to the rounded, softer lines of the Beetle-based Coupé. No one questioned that the new body was aesthetically balanced; its elongated front boot complemented the equally stretched and gently sloping rear. Stunningly large windows gave the Karmann Ghia 1500 owners more than pretensions of luxury. Its sharply inclined front screen and equally sloped rear window couldn't be compared with anything readily available on the European market,

Did the razor-edge styling do the KG 1500 any favours?

configured arrangement of headlamps. It was in these lines, which gained prominence once more towards the car's rear, that the nickname of 'razor-edge' was conceived. Their abrupt nosedive into the front bumper also helped in this respect.

While one cynical author has condemned the Karmann Ghia 1500's design as 'stolid', this was not its ongoing problem. The truth of the matter was that it was never exported to the USA, despite the fact that a few early examples made their way across the Atlantic for publicity purposes. Europeans undoubtedly preferred the classic elegance of the original Coupé and curiously, so too did the Americans, even buying it in preference to the Karmann Ghia 1500 semi-lookalikes from other manufacturers, which were soon readily available to them on the forecourts.

Although 140mm longer than the original Coupé, the Karmann Ghia 1500 varied little in width, with just a 10mm shortfall on its sister car's overall dimension. However, it had the advantage in terms of interior space, thanks to its more up-to-date styling technology. Height-wise the new car was 10mm taller, but it also sat closer to the ground (138mm compared to 172mm). In most other aspects, the two Karmann Ghias were more or less the same. Both offered two-plus-two seating, although there was a little more headroom in the Karmann Ghia 1500 for rear seat passengers. Both had more than one 'boot'. One was of a universal design at the front of the cars, while both cars shared the facility to tip the rear seats, creating additional luggage space. Only the Karmann Ghia 1500 had a purpose-built luggage compartment above the engine, a feature of all models however loosely associated with the Type 3 range.

Mechanically, the Karmann Ghia 1500 was identical to the other members of the VW 1500 family, but thanks to its more aerodynamic shape and reduction in weight, 2756lb compared to 2822lb for the VW 1500 Sedan, it could outperform both the rest of the Type 3 range and its Beetle-powered sister. According to Volkswagen, the Karmann Ghia 1500 had a top speed of 82mph, while the VW 1500 Sedan ran out of steam at 78mph, with the 0-50mph time varying by one second in the Karmann Ghia's favour.

let alone that of the original Coupé. What Ghia's Sergio Sartorelli had done was to create a vision – a car intended to provoke excitement in US hotspots.

Most distinctive of all was the Karmann Ghia 1500's frontal appearance, dominated by swage lines that culminated as a hood, or eyebrow, for the car's unusually

Hot news

Motoring journalists were eager to get behind the wheel of the Karmann Ghia 1500; the most exclusive and expensive model in the new VW 1500 range. As their reports began to appear on the pages of their magazines, Volkswagen and Karmann should have been particularly pleased. If their predictions were anything to go by, the Karmann Ghia 1500 was destined to be a big hit. Even those who might be expected to be sceptical, like *Road and Track*, had something kind to say:

'The first point to discuss might be the question of beauty. Some people like the newcomer very much, whereas others have not a single kind word for it – the rear end is accepted by most, but the front end ... has been the object of much controversy. One thing seems certain. Beautiful or not, giving the car the "different" look was a compulsory design target which – not many will doubt this – was accomplished. ... The style is distinctive, the price buys good quality and the privilege of being different – he who likes this combination will probably become a pleased owner, with the added, comfortable, knowledge that this very model is likely to remain in production, unchanged for many years to come.' *Road and Track*, February 1963

Car and Driver's contribution of January 1962 was unquestionably one of the most glowing: 'Volkswagen has never made any claims that the Ghia is a sports car – and neither would we. It is sporty however, and should appeal to a great number of people seeking pleasurable driving in an attractive package ... The Ghia is Volkswagen's concept of Grand Touring for two. It's made for people possessing a sophisticated automotive design sense (both aesthetic and technical), people who want to go places quickly and efficiently in an atmosphere of sporty good taste at a realistic fee.'

Other publications were less enamoured, but still full of praise: '... the most handsome VW so far ... the most desirable also ... good performance and handling. The 1.5 litre Karmann-Ghia is not a sports car – let's be clear on that point. Despite the beautiful line (I except the voluptuous front swoops), it is not a true racer, even by road standards. What's more important is the fact that it gives the driver a feeling he is rapid without getting him in trouble. ... the VW 1500KG is desirable in a way I haven't found amongst the flat-four clan.' *Cars Illustrated*, January 1963

Think of it.
As easily serviced as a Volkswagen.
Like all Volkswagen-made cars,
the Karmann Ghia 1500 was designed and
built to be serviced efficiently.
Quickly. And economically.
Engine and gear box, for example,
ride in a subframe that unbolts
in minutes. (Instead of removing
the engine to get at the gear box,
the mechanic removes the subframe.)
Lubrication takes only a few minutes.
Eight pressure points grease the entire car.
Parts are easy to get.
Authorized Volkswagen Dealers have them.
Labour charges are reasonable.
VW mechanics are factory-trained.
They know how to service and
inspect your car properly.
(And they don't waste time admiring
the workmanship; they've known about
Volkswagen-made cars for years.)

Gently evolving

Like other members of the air-cooled family, the Karmann Ghia 1500 evolved gently. In line with the VW 1500 on which it was based, there were some changes exclusively made to the Karmann Ghia 1500. However, nothing dramatic was contemplated in an attempt to boost or revitalise sales.

Mass production – if you could ever call it that – of the Karmann Ghia 1500 started in November 1961. In July 1962, a sunroof model was added to the line-up, perhaps as it was realised that the much talked of convertible version wasn't ever going to become a reality. Made out of steel, the sunroof operated electrically, working from a switch that was positioned below the cigarette lighter. Later in the same year, modifications were made to both the seatback adjustment and the doors, a change in this case which affected the quarter lights.

To coincide with the launch of the VW 1500S in August 1963, the Karmann Ghia was similarly upgraded. The twin carburettor engine, developing 54bhp, became the only option, while tyres were suitably upgraded to cope with the advance in power. Although it was well known for Volkswagen to alternate between horn buttons and semicircular rings

– in this instance the former being regarded as the latest advance – the change in design of the original rectangular bonnet badge to the more normal, round offering seems unnecessary. Good news, however, for those in Britain and other right-hand drive markets, was the addition of the Type 344 – or Karmann Ghia 1500 with the steering wheel on the right – to the range.

A year later, luxury was on the agenda, with new interior designs and colours on offer. A make-up mirror was offered to the front seat passenger and carpeting replaced rubber mats. Two-speed wipers made visibility easier in poor driving conditions, while an optional rear-window defroster helped on chilly nights. Another extra at added cost was a set of alloy wheel rings.

For the '67 model year – in addition to the 1584cc engine introduced twelve months earlier – the handbrake control became shorter and the gearlever was relocated. Either becoming predictably trendy or going upmarket, a wood-grain finish on the dashboard was offered. For the '68 model year, both automatic transmission and fuel injection were on offer.

Victim of the end of the Golden Age?

Had Nordhoff lived to see the seventies, would the larger Karmann Ghia Coupé have survived the axe that fell on it at the end of July 1969, with just 42,498 cars sold in a run spanning less than eight years?

In its first full year of production, 8541 Karmann Ghia 1500s had been produced, nearly 4000 units more than the Cabriolet version of the smaller Beetle-based 'sports' car, but only a little over 45 per cent of the ever-popular Coupé. A year later, the situation became worse at a sickly 29 per cent, a figure that virtually stayed the same in 1964. The following year saw figures of 6873 against 28,387 in the smaller Coupé's favour (24 per cent), while the recession year of 1967 saw a drop to just 2819 Karmann Ghia 1600s, a position from which it never recovered.

The lack of sales, for what had originally been predicted as a long-lived,

popular design, can be blamed on several factors. As already mentioned, the larger Karmann failed to make its way onto the lucrative US market, despite its appearance being far more suited to US (rather than conservative European) tastes. Likewise, although the car was bigger than the Beetle-based Karmann, it wasn't obvious to would-be buyers – neither car could legitimately be described as a full four-seater. Both had two boots, but lacked good luggage space, unless their bench-like rear seats were folded down. Initially at least, the Karmann Ghia 1500 had a reasonable advantage over the smaller car in terms of performance, but as the years went by this too was steadily eroded, despite

the introduction of the 1600 engine. The narrowing differences were never recognised by Volkswagen, at least in terms of price, which inevitably lead to potential customers going for what they perceived as the more elegant of the two Karmann vehicles. With that in mind, how could the Karmann Ghia 1600 hope to compete with what was, and many would argue still is, the most elegant car that Volkswagen had produced?

Some have suggested that the joint project VW-Porsche, built by Karmann and launched in the autumn of 1969 at the Frankfurt show, was a long planned successor to the Type 34 Karmann Ghia. Certainly Nordhoff and Ferry Porsche had decided to work together on the production of an affordable two-seater sports car. Volkswagen was only too aware that in the USA 12,000 examples of the MGB could be sold annually. Although Nordhoff saw the proposed mid-engine design in 1967, the first prototype was only available to view on March 1 1968, just fifteen days before he collapsed and less than a month before the great man's death. Therefore it was his successor, Kurt Lotz, who gave the green light.

Nordhoff had cancelled projects at the last moment in the past. Massively more expensive than the Karmann Ghia 1600, although definitely more powerful, it seems quite likely that if Nordhoff had sanctioned production, it would have been as an additional model in the range, rather than as a Karmnan Ghia 1600 replacement. In just over twenty years at the top, Nordhoff didn't withdraw a single car from his slowly extending range. It might be that the Karmann Ghia 1600 would have continued in production for no other reasons than either failure being blinkered out, or the basic package being sound with merely the trimmings of success absent. We shall never know ...

VW 411
Legacy of a Golden Age

'The fastest, most exciting and most comfortable car ever to come from Volkswagen.' That's how the marketing team described the VW 411, launched in October 1968, six months after Nordhoff's death, but very much a product of his age and his final legacy.

Long the subject of sneak preview photos, the VW 411 bore a passing resemblance to the VW 1600TL, while Pininfarina, who had an advisory contract with Wolfsburg, was credited with the car's styling. With an overall length of 4525mm, the VW 411 was 157mm longer than the VW 1600, but the cars were virtually identical in width. The wheelbase was 2500mm. What was unique at the time for Volkswagen was that it had a 'unitised all-steel body' (Transporters don't qualify here). Gone were the days of separate floor pans. Volkswagen were eager to point out that it had 'the

same chassis as the Porsche 911. The same suspension struts ... the same double-joint rear axle'. Out had gone the trailing link front axle with torsion bars; in came track control arms – MacPherson struts located to the body with torsion bars and double-acting telescopic shock absorbers. Perhaps double-joint rear axles had already become the preference, but out went the torsion bars again, replaced by trailing wishbones and coil springs over double-acting telescopic shock absorbers. Thanks to these innovations, cornering was more neutral, while, by dropping any serious notion of a boot over the engine, a weight distribution of 45/55 was achieved.

The marketing men described the VW 411's traditional flat-four, air-cooled, boxer engine as 'powerful'. With twin Solex carburettors, the 1679cc engine developed 76bhp

and reached maximum torque at 3300rpm. The copywriters added that this arrangement made 'it flexible with plenty of poke at low speeds', and noted that it was the reason 'you can accelerate from 0-50 in 11.5 secs'. Maximum and cruising speed were the same, coming in at a beefy 90mph. However, Nordhoff's legacy was apparent in an emphasis on robustness and durability – the 'completely new design' had pistons and cylinders that were wider than they were long. 'In other words, the engine is extremely over-square. The stroke is short and piston speed low'.

The VW 411 had all the necessary ingredients to make both a successful bigger family car and to appeal to those with aspirations of opulence. After all, it was the first model, at least in its Sedan form, to be offered with four or two doors. Its fully lined front boot amounted to 14cu ft – 'room and to

spare for five-good sized cases'. The brochure compilers claimed that 'luxurious is the only word to describe the equipment in the VW 411', and waxed lyrical about the lack of a central tunnel and seats that could be adjusted both up and down, as well as fore and aft. They went to town with the Eberspächer petrol-electrical auxiliary heater, 'which keeps you toasty warm en route. No matter how hot you like it. And which even heats if the engine isn't running.' The fresh-air ventilation was aided by a two-speed electric blower – 'No draughts. No noise. Just fresh air.'

Initially only available as a Sedan, two levels of trim were offered, the 'L' including such extravagances as velour upholstery, as opposed to the usual vinyl. The VW 411 could also be specified with a sliding sunroof, or as a full automatic.

To many, the VW 411's progress (or lack of it) will be well known. From reactions like *Auto, Motor und Sport* that it was 'attractive and well equipped, offering four passengers plenty of room', rumours soon began to circulate of the new director general referring to the car as something considerably less than a 'metal Adonis'. In years to come, in an attempt to rectify the falling profits and poor sales of those cars that Lotz wished to succeed, he would price such products at a level intended to stimulate growth, without considering the effect on Nordhoff's largest Volkswagen. Truly, the first Golden Age was over.

List of featured brochures

1938, *KdF-Wagen*
1951, *Der Kleinbus*
1953, *Beetle Untitled*
1954, *Volkswagen's wide range of commercial vehicles*
1956, *The Convertible*
1956, *Beetle Untitled*
1957, *Die VW-Transporter*
1957, *Karmann Ghia*
1958, *Karmann Ghia*
1958, *Volkswagen The Honest Car*
1958, *Volkswagen The Honest Car (Version 2)*
1959, *The Volkswagen Transporters*
1959, *Getting Ahead with VW Trucks*
1959, *The Volkswagen Transporters - The wide range*
1959, *For business or pleasure VW Station Wagons*
1959, *Volkswagen Karmann Ghia*
1960, *Which is the shape of VW trucks to come?*
1961, *Beetle Das automobil des vernunftigen fortschritts*
1961, *Meet the Volkswagen Truck*
1961, *VW Ambulance*
1962, *VW 1500*
1962, *The new VW1500 Convertible*
1962, *VW 1500 Karmann Ghia*
1963, *Volkswagen 1200*
1963, *Volkswagen Standard Limousine*
1963, *Open the door (KG)*
1963, *All about the VW 1500*
1963, *What kind of car is a Volkswagen?*
1964, *What makes a Volkswagen a Volkswagen?*

1964, *Presenting America's slowest fastback*
1964, *Why is the Volkswagen a favourite in 136 Countries?*
1964, *Wie vielseitig ...*
1965, *Our School Bus - Safely to School*
1965, *Sure as night follows day*
1965, *The VW idea in the 1.5litre class 1500S*
1966, *You want to buy a new car in the 1000-1300cc range?*
1966, *Transporter (Crates)*
1966, *What's the VW Commercial got to write home about?*
1966, *What have you got when you've got a VW 1600TL*
1966, *A hardworking Devon motor caravan*
1967, *Waarom is de Volkswagen in 136 landen zo geliefd*
1967, *Now the VW1300 is also available with a 1.5litre engine*
1967, *The New VW 1200 -The best VW ever made*
1967, *Transport efficiently and travel comfortably*
1967, *The Canterbury Moto Caravan*
1967, *The new VW Commercial*
1967, *Why is the Volkswagen so popular in 136 countries?*
1968, *Introducing the new VW 1600S with auto transmission*
1968, *Die Neuen Kafer*
1969, *Their good looks are the least important thing about*
1969, *The VW 411. Just put your present car alongside it*

Bibliography

Getting the Bugs Out, David Kiley, John Wiley, 2002
Karmann Ghia 1955 1982, R M Clarke (Compiler), Brooklands Books, 1985
Original VW Beetle, Laurence Meredith, Bay View, 1994
Original VW Bus, Laurence Meredith, Bay View, 1997
Remember those great VW ads?, Abbott & Marcantonio, Europe Illust, 1982
Small Wonder, Walter Henry Nelson, Hutchinson, 1970
The Beetle, Keith Seume, CLB Int, 1997
The Beetle - Design and Evolution Vol 2, Hans Rudiger Etzold, Haynes, 1990
The Beetle - Production and Evolution Vol 1, Hans Rudiger Etzold, Haynes, 1988
The VW Beetle, Robin Fry, David & Charles, 1980
The VW Story, Jerry Sloniger, Stephens, 1980
Volkswagen Beetle, Sueme & Shaill, Bay View, 1993
Volkswagen Beetle Model by Model, Laurence Meredith, Crowood, 1999
Volkswagen Cars and Trucks, Keith Seume, MBI Publishing, 2001
Volkswagen Chronicle, Volkswagen AG Group Coms, 2003
Volkswagen Model History, Joachim Kuch, Haynes, 1999
Volkswagen Transporter, Laurence Meredith, Crowood, 1998
Volkswagens of the World, Simon Glenn, Veloce, 1999
VW A Brief Illustrated History, Volkswagenwerk AG, 1979
VW Beetle 1956-1977, R M Clarke (Compiler), Brooklands Bks
VW Beetle. The Car of the 20th Century, Richard Copping, Veloce, 2001
VW Bus, Malcolm Bobbitt, Veloce, 1998
VW Karmann Ghia, Malcolm Bobbitt, Veloce, 1995
VW Transporter and Microbus, David Eccles, Crowood, 2002

More from Veloce Publishing ...

The Essential Buyer's Guide
VOLKSWAGEN
BEETLE

Your marque experts: Ken Cservenka & Richard Copping

ISBN 978-1-904788-72-0

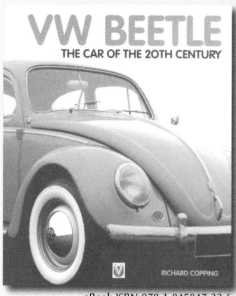

VW BEETLE
THE CAR OF THE 20TH CENTURY

RICHARD COPPING

eBook ISBN 978-1-845847-32-6

NEW EDITION

Volkswagen
Beetle Cabriolet

The full story of the convertible Beetle

Malcolm Bobbitt

ISBN 978-1-845840-74-7

ENTHUSIAST'S RESTORATION MANUAL

How to restore
Volkswagen Beetle

YOUR step-by-step illustrated guide to body, trim & mechanical restoration
All models 1953 to 2003

Jim Tyler

ISBN 978-1-845849-46-7